AF366941

A Global Approach to the Gender Gap in Mathematical, Computing, and Natural Sciences

How to Measure It, How to Reduce It?

Edited by

Colette Guillopé and Marie-Françoise Roy

Gender Gap in Science project

Final report

The project *A Global Approach to the Gender Gap in Mathematical, Computing, and Natural Sciences: How to Measure It, How to Reduce It?* was made possible by funding from the International Science Council.

This is the final version of the report.
`https://gender-gap-in-science.org/`.

Cartoons and cover illustration: Léa Castor
Book design and layout: Christian Steinfeldt

ISBN 978-3-00-065533-3

Contents

Measuring and analyzing the gender gap in science through the joint data-backed study on publication patterns   83

Helena Mihaljević, Lucía Santamaría

Some initiatives for reducing the gender gap in science: a database of good practices

155

Regina Kelly, Merrilyn Goos

Impact of the Gender Gap in Science project in Africa, Asia and Latin America

177

Silvina Ponce Dawson, Igle Gledhill, Mei-Hung Chiu

Report of the final conference of the Gender Gap in Science project   **195**

Colette Guillopé, Marie-Françoise Roy

Preface

The gender, diversity and inclusion dimension of science and technology has become a highly visible and debated theme worldwide, impacting society at every level. A variety of international initiatives have been undertaken, and a vast number of international organizations have made clear statements about their anti-discrimination policies, including the International Science Council (ISC), whose regulations are followed by all its member unions. *"Achieve gender equality and empower all women and girls"* is also one of the seventeen United Nations Sustainable Development Goals[1], which clearly calls for action related to the gender gap in science and technology.

While the number of women undertaking higher education studies in STEM (Science, Technology, Engineering and Mathematics) fields steadily increases, women continue to lag behind when they start their professional careers. The persistence of the disparity between women holding PhDs in science and women at the junior faculty level shows that the problem won't solve itself. Targeted actions are still very much needed to address the under representation of women in STEM beyond the student years. Most of the interest and action has so far come from discipline-based societies or highly committed political entities.

Therefore, we are very proud to present this report that focuses on the results of our three-years' project *A Global Approach to the Gender Gap in Mathematical and Natural Sciences: How to Measure It, How to Reduce It?* For the first time, seven scientific unions in STEM domains and four international organizations joined forces to tackle some specific aspects of the gender gap. In terms of interdisciplinarity, this has been a unique initiative and collaborative effort. The project was co-led by the International Mathematical Union (IMU) and the International Union of Pure and Applied Chemistry (IUPAC), with the financial support guaranteed by ISC and the project partners over the triennium 2017–2019.

---

[1]United Nations Sustainable Development Goals,
https://www.un.org/sustainabledevelopment/.

The project was aimed to better understand the issues facing mathematical, computing, and natural science academics and practitioners around the world. It has consisted of three main tasks: *i.)* A Joint Global Survey that was launched in May 2018, which stayed open until December 2018, and to which more than 30,000 individuals responded; *ii.)* A detailed investigation of gender patterns in millions of scientific publications; *iii.)* The setting-up of a best-practice database of initiatives that address the gender gap in Mathematical, Computing, and Natural Sciences at various levels.

Three years are rather short for the achievement of these ambitious goals. The project has faced several challenges, in terms of time-pressure, technical and human issues, but the enthusiasm and commitment of its partners has done the magic. We engaged in all aspects of this initiative and have learned a lot together and from one another. The opportunity to discuss pros and cons of the various initiatives and policies implemented by the individual partners has been very rewarding and has undoubtedly enriched us all. The three regional meetings in Colombia, South Africa and Taiwan and the final conference at the International Centre of Theoretical Physics in Italy, organized by the project, have been very successful in terms of participants' response, for their enthusiasm, engagement, and active contribution across the many interactive sessions.

Based on the findings of the project tasks and discussions held within the network that formed around the project, we have proposed recommendations for different audiences: instructors and parents, scientific or educational organizations of all kinds, and the members of the project, which are Scientific Unions and worldwide organizations.

We hope that this report and its recommendations will inspire you as much as they are inspiring us. We warmly thank those of you who have supported us by responding to the Joint Global Survey – without your commitment we would have not been able to assemble such a broad picture of what an education and a profession in STEM imply in terms of challenges and obstacles, for both men and women.

The path to gender equality in the STEM fields is still uphill, but this project has pushed us one step further and with the data, results and tools created by our project, we will be able to draw effective and tailored policies for the future.

Marie-Françoise Roy,

　　　　on behalf of *International Mathematical Union (IMU)*

Mei-Hung Chiu,

　　　on behalf of *International Union of Pure and Applied Chemistry (IUPAC)*

Irvy (Igle) Gledhill,

　　　on behalf of *International Union of Pure and Applied Physics (IUPAP)*

Francesca Primas,

　　　　on behalf of *International Astronomical Union (IAU)*

Nathalie Fomproix,

　　　on behalf of *International Union of Biological Sciences (IUBS)*

Jean Taylor,

　　on behalf of *International Council for Industrial and Applied Mathematics (ICIAM)*

Catherine Jami,

 on behalf of *International Union of History and Philosophy of Science and Technology (IUHPST)*

Peggy Oti-Boateng,

　on behalf of *United Nations Educational, Scientific and Cultural Organization (UNESCO)*

Roseanne Diab,

　　on behalf of *Gender in Science, Innovation, Technology and Engineering (GenderInSite)*

Tonya Blowers,

　　on behalf of *Organization of Women in Science for the Developing World (OWSD)*

Jodi Tims,

　　　on behalf of *Association for Computing Machinery (ACM)*

A Global Approach to the Gender Gap
in Mathematical, Computing, and Natural Sciences:
RESULTS AND RECOMMENDATIONS

A Global Approach to the Gender Gap in Mathematical, Computing, and Natural Sciences: Results and Recommendations

Marie-Françoise Roy[1], Colette Guillopé[2], Mark Cesa[3]

1 – Chair of the International Mathematical Union Committee for Women in Mathematics
2 – French Association Women & Science, Honor President
3 – 2014–2015 President, International Union of Pure and Applied Chemistry, markcesa@comcast.net

The aim of this chapter is to give a summary presentation of our Gender Gap in Science interdisciplinary project.

We first define the gender gap in science and explain the various methodologies used within the project to measure it, analyze it and design initiatives to reduce it. The first task of the project, the Global Survey of Scientists, examined how the experiences of women and men in science differ around the world, building on previous similar studies for physicists [2]. In the second task, where we studied the difference in publication patterns for women and men, we generalize and extend prior research done in Mathematics. In the database of good practices, we build tools to present and analyze some of the many initiatives deployed to reduce the gender gap in science. We also report on another important aspect of our activities, the organization of three regional workshops, in Africa, Asia and Latin America, and of the final Conference held at the International Centre for Theoretical Physics (ICTP). Finally, the results of the project, the tools produced and the activities we organized are summarized briefly, with much more precise information being given in the subsequent chapters.

This chapter ends with the main recommendations identified through the project and how we envision the future of the project.

Gender gap and project goals

What is meant by gender gap?

The term "gender gap" describes any difference

"between women and men in terms of their levels of participation, access, rights, remuneration or benefits." [1]

It is usually analyzed and measured through various specific indicators. The Global Gender Gap Index (GGGI), for instance, aims to measure this gap in four key areas: health, education, economics and politics.[1] The Global Gender Gap Report is published annually by the World Economic Forum since 2006 and ranks countries according to the value of their GGGI.

What about the gender gap in science?

According to the UNESCO Institute for Statistics (UIS) fewer than 30% of the world's researchers are women, which reflects a clear gender gap in science.[2] But to truly understand and reduce the gender gap, it is necessary to go beyond these numbers and identify the various factors that deter women from pursuing careers or succeeding in Science, Technology, Engineering and Mathematics (STEM).

Defining and describing accurately the gender gap in science requires a good understanding of how the scientific community is organized. This differs from one discipline to another, and from continent to continent. Therefore we are also presenting many results independent of gender, since without this context it is difficult to adequately interpret

---

[1]World Economic Forum, *The Global Gender Gap Index 2020*,
```
http://reports.weforum.org/global-gender-gap-report-2020/
the-global-gender-gap-index-2020/.
```
[2]UNESCO Institute for Statistics, *Women in Science*,
```
http://uis.unesco.org/en/topic/women-science
```

Figure 1: The scientific community: only 30% women.

the results; it is only in conjunction with the whole, ungendered picture of a scientific discipline that insights about the particular role of women can emerge.

What distinguishes your project from the numerous other projects or publications addressing the gender gap?

Indeed, there is intensive research on the gender gap in science and a lot of literature has already been published.

Our project is distinct from prior works in several ways. First, its scope is global rather than restricted to a specific part of the world. It is also multidisciplinary rather than restricted to one discipline. Another specificity is that, though it will result in several research publications, and the bulk of the work has been done by professionals, the project leaders are a combination of scientists and specialists of gender gap related issues.

Eleven organizations have joined their efforts. Seven of these are union members of the International Science Council: namely the International Mathematical Union (IMU) through its Committee for Women in Mathematics; the International Union of Pure and Applied Chemistry (IUPAC); the International Union of Pure and Applied Physics (IUPAP); the International Astronomical Union (IAU), the International Union of Biological Sciences (IUBS); the International Council for Industrial and Applied Mathematics (ICIAM); and the International Union of History and Philosophy of Science and Technology (IUHPST). The other four organizations are the United Nations Educational, Scientific and Cultural Organization (UNESCO), through its project STEM and Gender

Advancement (SAGA); Gender in Science, Innovation, Technology and Engineering (GenderInSITE); the Organization of Women in Science for the Developing World (OWSD); and the Association for Computing Machinery (ACM), through ACM-W.

The originality of the project also comes from combining various methodologies. In the first aspect of the project, the Global Survey of Scientists, we updated and extended the 2009 Global Survey of Physicists [2], which examined the experiences of women and men in Physics around the world. In the publication patterns, we extracted information from existing databases of scientific publications, generalizing and extending prior research done in Mathematics. In the database of good practices we built a conceptual framework to present and analyze some of the many initiatives invented to reduce the gender gap in science.

What aspects of the gender gap in science are addressed through your project?

Through our study of publication patterns, we have provided significant insights on the gender gap as defined by various aspects known to be relevant for the advancement of academic careers. These include

- the proportion of women as scientific authors,

- comparisons of the so-called publication dropout rates, which are good proxies of scientists' career lengths,

- the productivity gap, which examines the amount of research output per gender, and provides a frequently used argument against promotion or tenure of women,

- the presence of women as authors in renowned journals.

All these aspects have been presented in our analyses in a thorough way for the disciplines we were able to study, over significant periods of time. The analysis of renowned journals and the question about the large observed gender gap among their published authors might become particularly relevant, as science policy decision makers in some countries have started to shift the focus away from quantity of publications to their quality, which is typically measured by the prestige of the publishing venue.

Through the Global Survey of Scientists we have addressed several aspects that are not measurable via bibliographic metadata, such as issues related to missing role models, feelings of critical exclusion, harassment, or low participation and retention rates. The

Figure 2: We *do* love science.

Global Survey of Scientists assesses scientists' experiences (male and female) throughout their careers. More precisely, the survey reveals how scientists perceived the early years of their education, university studies, doctoral studies, and careers, whether they experienced discrimination or sexual harassment. The questions in the survey addressed the following aspects: development of interest in science, experiences in education and careers, work-life balance, family support, access to resources needed to conduct science, and opportunities to contribute to the scientific enterprise.

Many initiatives all over the world have been designed to reduce the gender gap, but very few of them provide evidence of effectiveness and impact. This is the reason why we developed a database of good practices and introduced a conceptual framework to analyze them.

Methodologies

In the Global Survey of Scientists you used a snowball technique. Can you explain the method, tell us why you used it and explain its advantages and inconveniences?

Figure 3: Women in science all around the world.

In statistical research, snowball sampling is a technique where existing study subjects recruit future subjects from among their contacts. Thus the sample group is said to grow like a rolling snowball.

We collected data using a snowball sampling method and used contact databases from some partnering organizations to reach students and professional scientists across the globe. Since there is not a single network or resource available to contact all students and professional scientists globally, we used snowball sampling to take advantage of as many personal networks as possible.

Snowball sampling is a non-probability method for data collection and does not result in a statistically representative sample. Because of this, there are important limitations in analysis and interpretation for the data collected by the survey. Therefore, our findings only indicate trends among the individuals who responded to the survey, not the overall population.

Summarizing, the findings presented in this report should not be assumed to be representative of the intended population as a whole. However, the consistency of most of our findings across disciplines, geographical zones and development level is reassuring.

In our Global Survey, some of our partners (particularly in Mathematics or Physics) had a more active network with respect to Women in Science or Gender Equality than other partners, so that the proportions of answers do not reflect the respective weight of the disciplines participating in the project in terms of number of scientists. Even so, our analysis techniques allow us to make statements about the relative experiences of men and women in multiple disciplines, working in different sectors, and studying and pursuing careers worldwide.

What are the statistical tools that you used in the analysis of the data collected with the Global Survey of Scientists?

In this final report of the project, we focus on multivariate analyses. The multivariate analyses allow the identification of potential confounding factors, such as employment sector, discipline, geographic region, age, and more, in the analysis. We are still able to conclude that there are statistically significant differences in the responses of men and women after accounting for potential confounding factors. Moreover, the difference between men and women is often more significant in this multivariate approach, compared to the initial bivariate results obtained earlier in the project.

Your second methodology is focussed on publication patterns. Why are publication patterns relevant for understanding the gender gap in science?

Successful academic careers are strongly tied to a prolific scholarly record; scientific publications are not only the major outlet for scholarly communication, they are regarded as a proxy for a researcher's scientific credentials and play a key role in achieving and maintaining a successful career in academia. Decisions on tenure and other academic promotions are mostly based on evaluations of the candidate's research portfolio that pay special attention to research publications like journal articles, grants, conference presentations, and the visibility or renown of the scholar. Thus, the understanding of publication practices in various cientific disciplines, obtained through measurable data on research output, is of great interest to academic institutions, science policy makers, and researchers alike [4, 3].

Moreover, examining exhaustive data sources gives a full picture of the situation and offers the opportunity to undertake longitudinal studies.

What disciplines have you studied in the publication analyses and what data sources have you used?

The selection of disciplines is limited by the availability of suitable data sources, which must be accessible (preferably via open data or at least operated by a scientific institution),

Figure 4: Publish or perish.

represent a discipline comprehensively and provide sufficiently good data quality. Through established cooperation we gained access to the representative high-quality databases zb-MATH for publications in Mathematics and ADS (Astronomy Data System) for literature in Astronomy and Astrophysics. Furthermore, we used the data of the open access e-print archive arXiv to study publication patterns in Theoretical Physics. In order to better explore the participation of women as authors in well-known journals, we enriched the arXiv data with the database CrossRef. Additionally, we retrieved data from CrossRef for selected renowned chemistry journals, since we had no access to a comprehensive data source for Chemistry.

What are the methods you used to identify female authors?

Bibliographic metadata do not include the authors' gender, so this information had to be inferred. Usually, an author's name is the only piece of information that can dprovide an indication of gender. For the present data we have combined responses from different gender assignment services that we had benchmarked as part of the project. As a result of the gender assignment procedure, all author names are tagged as "female", "male", or "unknown".

Plenty of issues arise in connection with Automated Gender Recognition (AGR). Names are not always "uniquely" associated to one gender, which leads to a bias towards certain countries. For instance, authors of Chinese ancestry are more often assigned unknown labels due to loss of "gender marking" during transliteration. Furthermore, all AGR approaches, building on names or other physiological features, such as facial images or voice, only allow for a binary definition of gender, which fundamentally excludes individuals who do not conform to this societal concept. Despite these issues, we have performed a name-based gender recognition because gender differences can be observed in various aspects of academic life and need to be explained.

Main Results

How many answers did you get to the survey?

There were 32,346 respondents from 159 countries, half male and half female.

What are the key findings of the survey?

The results of the survey confirm that the Gender Gap in Science is very real, across all regions, all disciplines, and development levels. Women's experiences in both educational and employment settings are consistently less positive than men's.

In particular, over a quarter of women respondents across the sciences reported personally experiencing sexual harassment at school or work. Our multivariate analysis finds that women were over 14 times more likely than men to report being personally harassed; this analysis accounts for discipline, age, employment sector, geographic region, and level of development. This is strong evidence that men and women have different experiences with harassment. Women were also statistically more likely than men to say they had personally witnessed sexual harassment.

Across all regions, all disciplines, and all levels of development, women were significantly more likely than men to report discrimination based on gender. Women are less likely than men to report respectful treatment by co-workers.

Women were 1.6 times more likely than men to report interruptions in their studies, a major factor in successful completion of university studies that is connected to the ability of a student to engage in continuous studies. Women reported less positive relationships

Figure 5: A mountain of obstacles.

with their doctoral advisors, and lower doctoral program quality. They were less likely than men to say that everyone is treated fairly in the educational system and in employment.

There continues to be a salary gap between women and men in the sciences. We have included potential explanatory factors including age (as a proxy for career progress), discipline, geographic region, employment sector, and level of human development. Even after accounting for these factors, we find that women were more likely to report lower pay compared to colleagues with similar qualifications. Women reported less access to career-advancing resources and opportunities than men. They were more likely than men to report slower career progression than their peers.

Becoming a parent had significantly different impacts on the lives of women and men. For example, we found that women were more likely to say that their career progression slowed after having their first child.

Figure 6: Working in a male environment.

Overall, women were more likely than men to say that they relied on their personal determination, will power, and hard work for their success in science. They were also more likely than men to report being encouraged during their university studies by their spouse or partner, parents, and other family members. It is the most significant instance where the situation of women is reported as better than that of men. Maybe this means that without strong personal determination and significant encouragement by their relatives, women are less likely to become scientists.

What does the survey say about the gender gap in various disciplines?

In spite of very different situations with respect to the proportions of women in the various disciplines (less than 30% in Mathematics, more than 50% in Biology) the key findings of the Survey are very similar across the various disciplines.

What can you say about the gender gap with respect to development levels?

The main conclusion is that there is a gender gap in science both for more developed and less developed countries. The gender gap in science does not disappear with increasing economic or even human development (as defined by the Human Development Index (HDI)). In some instances, a higher level of development is even correlated with a more

Figure 7: Same job, different pay.

negative experience by the respondents in terms of graduate program quality, relationship with one's graduate advisor, and personal harassment.

What can you say about the gender gap in various geographic zones?

To take an example, the lowest rate of interruptions in higher education studies was reported in Western Europe, possibly because the social system is more supportive there.

Given that the Global Survey of Scientists appears as an extension of the Survey of Physicists realized in a previous project, is there any opportunity to draw conclusions using a longitudinal study?

Given the snowball methodology used, we cannot draw conclusions. However, results from the Survey of Physicists [2] in 2009 and the Global Survey of Scientists (with several scientific disciplines) in 2018 are strikingly similar.

Are there other important findings emerging from the Global Survey of Scientists that you would like to mention?

We did obtain interesting results, independent of our main gender gap focus. We have compared the answers from the various disciplines and employment sectors, after

Figure 8: Career progression?

accounting for potential confounding factors including age, gender, employment sector, geographic region, and HDI, but we believe further research is needed for insight into these differences.

In examining doctoral programs, we found that respondents studying Mathematics had a more positive perception of their advisor relationship than respondents in other disciplines. Respondents studying Computer Science, Mathematics, and Physics were more likely than those in other disciplines to perceive they had been treated fairly in their graduate programs. In examining employment sectors, respondents working in industry, NGOs, and primary/secondary schools were more likely to report being treated respectfully by co-workers than respondents working in academia or in the government sector. Respondents working in industry and NGOs were more likely to report being treated fairly by their employers than those working in the government sector.

How many references did you analyze in the Publication Pattern task?

We analyzed millions of references. To take an example, the zbMATH data set that we used to study publication patterns in mathematics comprises 3,083,185 documents corresponding to 5,273,035 instances of authorship.

Is there a reduction over time of the gender gap in publication patterns?

Drop-out rates, which used to be higher for women, are converging on similar values for both genders. For many years a "productivity gap" was observed: that is, there was a disparity in the academic performance of male and female researchers. The productivity gap is becoming narrower, although in recent cohorts this trend shows signs of stagnation. In Theoretical Physics and Mathematics, women from the cohorts 1995–2005 publish at a rate of 85–90% of the outputs of their male counterparts after 10 years of an active academic career. In Astronomy and Astrophysics the figures show an even more equal picture, with female astronomers publishing at a rate of 95% of the outputs men produce.

In the analyses of academic publications – did you observe any changes in authorships by women over time?

The answer is a clear yes. In Mathematics, it is remarkable to point out that the proportion of women among authors of scientific papers has increased steadily, growing from less than 10% for the 1970s cohorts to over 27% nowadays. And the evolution in Physics and Astronomy is similar.

How does the publication gender gap look like in various disciplines?

It is noteworthy that the proportion of women authoring papers in top journals has been significantly increasing in Astronomy and Astrophysics as well as in Chemistry. However, it remained static in various top journals in Mathematics and Theoretical Physics and at a very low level, beneath 10%, which is significantly below the overall proportion of women authoring papers.

There seems to exist a pattern of fewer women authors in theoretical disciplines and subdisciplines while a larger presence is found in applied and collaborative fields. The question therefore arises as to what role is played by research collaborations and to which extent larger academic networks help women's careers.

In which countries did you observe the highest proportions of women authors?

In Astronomy and Mathematics, the countries with the highest relative proportions of women are located in Europe. Germany and France have a significant scientific weight in both disciplines, in particular in Astronomy and Astrophysics. Countries in Eastern and Southeastern Europe are also relatively strong in terms of women's presence. Particularly notable are Italy, Turkey, Romania, and Balkan countries like Bulgaria, Serbia and Croatia.

The USA enjoys a leading position in the production of scientific research as a whole, and interestingly, the contribution of its female mathematicians and astronomers does not greatly deviate from the average ignoring gender. In South America the most positive

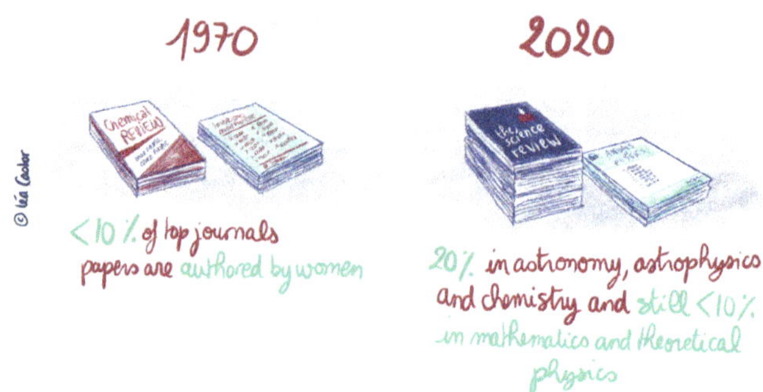

Figure 9: Evolution in top journals?

situation for women is found in Argentina. There are only very few countries from other continents with a relatively good representation of women: specifically, for the participation from Africa there is either too little data to provide meaningful statistics or women are strongly underrepresented, especially in Astronomy and Astrophysics. In Iran, India and China women represent a minority in both disciplines, but especially in Astronomy. In most Asian countries the presence of women is very small. A positive exception in both fields appears to come from Pakistan.

Given the aim of project, your study of publication patterns has been mainly directed at obtaining information on the gender gap in science. What can you say about Publication Patterns more generally?

Our methods make it possible to observe the evolution of publication patterns globally: the role of collaborations and the proportion of single author papers, the geographical distribution of scientific networks, and the diversity of practices among various disciplines. They open up a fascinating collection of research problems.

What was achieved in the Database of Good Practices for girls and young women, parents and organizations?

We have assembled a selection of initiatives for reducing the gender gap in many countries and disciplines. Moreover, we have developed a set of dimensions that in our assessment characterize "good practices" and applied these to the initiatives in an attempt to explain

Figure 10: Parents encourage math-learning daughter.

WHY they "work". These dimensions are based on the SAGA Science, Technology and Innovation Gender Objectives List (STI GOL) developed by UNESCO [5]. The SAGA list has seven dimensions of good practice that were originally created to classify policies rather than practices. Because our database is meant to assemble examples of "good practices", we modified the SAGA list by adding more subcategories in order to capture a broader and more relevant range of practical gender interventions.

Can you say something about good practices?

Good practices are multi-dimensional and address the gender gap in science across many contexts: in society; in school and vocational education; in higher education; in careers; and in research, policy-making and entrepreneurship. When we were searching for examples of good practices to include in the database, we found the highest proportion of examples within the first four of these categories. By far the most frequent type of initiative involved promoting STEM careers to girls and young women in school or vocational education contexts; for example, by stimulating interest, providing career information, and presenting role models. But simply telling females about STEM opportunities is unlikely to make a great difference to the gender gap, unless other supporting strategies are implemented. Four such strategies are illustrated in the subcategories that we added to the STI GOL list: (1) Engage families and communities in promoting STEM careers to girls, especially when these careers are contrary to cultural expectations and norms; (2) Engage females in exploring socio-scientific issues; (3) Promote social support for females, such as peer networks and mentoring by more experienced STEM researchers or professionals; and (4) Develop females' STEM leadership, advocacy and communication skills. Collectively, these additional "good practices" emphasize the need for support that is sensitive to girls' and young women's social and cultural contexts.

Tools produced

Where is it possible to see the questions of the Global Survey of Scientists?

- The questionnaire in several languages is available at:
  `https://statisticalresearchcenter.aip.org/global18`.
- The list of all the questions in English can be found at:
  `http://bit.ly/GSSQuestionList`.

Is it possible for researchers outside the project to access the data collected in the Global Survey of Scientists?

We have discussed internally how unions and organizations inside or outside the project could access the data. The issue is data privacy: individuals who answered the survey must not be identified. The solution we proposed initially was to have a committee that could assess proposals and provide access to the data under certain conditions, but those technological requirements are in almost no case assured. Recent technologies make it possible to protect the privacy of data while providing open access to researchers, so this is what we are exploring now and are considering implementing in the future.

Are the data and analyses on publication behaviour accessible to others? If so, in what form?

Our study is intended to be sustainable and aims at making data available to interested audiences. Thus, a major effort of our work has been to build and maintain an open platform that allows ad-hoc analyses of bibliographic data in relation to gender. The resulting webpage can be accessed via its public URL. The site provides structured access to publication data from STEM disciplines in relation to the gender of the publishing authors. Our visualizations address several crucial aspects for understanding the impact of publication patterns on the gender gap: research activity over time; women's share of publications in particular journals; and distribution across sub-fields.

The aim of the interactive platform is to encourage analyses that contribute to a better understanding of the interplay between scientists' gender and their scholarly output. By providing dynamic visualizations we wish to enable researchers, scientific organizations, policy makers, and interested members of the general public to explore the data, formulate new hypotheses, and derive evidence to inform their decision-making processes. The Gender Publication Gap website will continue to be available also after completion of the Gender Gap in Science Project.

Publication pattern study result website,

```
http://gender-publication-gap.f4.htw-berlin.de/.
```

What are the tools produced by the Database of Good Practices approach?

We produced a searchable database of good practices. Each initiative was classified according to its geographical origin, discipline, intended audience or target participants, dimensions of good practice, and evidence of effectiveness and impact, available at the IMU Committee for Women in Mathematics (CWM) website. It is possible for users to propose new initiatives to be added to the database and we wish to encourage such contributions in the future.

Database of Good Practices website,

```
https://www.mathunion.org/cwm/gender-gap-in-science-database.
```

During the first year of the project, you organized three regional meetings, in Africa, Asia and Latin America. What was their purpose?

The vision of the International Science Council (ISC), which is the main funding source for our project, is that science is a global public good. The ISC is fully committed to helping achieve the 17 ambitious goals of the 2030 Agenda for Sustainable Development of the

United Nations that aim, among other things, to reduce inequality and poverty. Gender equality is one of the 17 goals of the 2030 agenda. As stated by the UN,

> *"gender equality is not only a fundamental human right, but a necessary foundation for a peaceful, prosperous and sustainable world".*[3]

Sharing this vision, our Global Gender Gap in Science Project has worked towards exchanging knowledge and resources across the developing world, especially in the three regions where the ISC has regional offices: Africa, Asia and Latin America. So it was natural that one of the first activities of the project was the organization of workshops in these three regions to incorporate a global perspective into the organization of the project and build a network all over the world. This network proved to be very useful during the finalisation and dissemination phases of the Global Survey of Scientists.

What was the aim of the final conference at the International Centre for Theoretical Physics (ICTP) and what were its main achievements?

The first aim of the conference at ICTP was to report on the project's methodology, tools and results, and formulate recommendations and open questions based on its results. The invited talks were not intended to be speculative about the nature of the gender gap, but rather to refer to the results gathered and produced within the project. A second aim of this conference was to make it possible for attendees to learn how to use the tools of the project and answer their own questions.

In terms of participation, the conference was a huge success, with 102 participants (90 female and 12 male) while the original proposal as submitted to ICTP had anticipated 74 attendees only. There were 26 attendees from Africa, 15 from Asia, 36 from Europe, 11 from Latin America, 11 from North America and 3 from Oceania, with a total of 57 countries represented. This success is of course related to the initial networking effort through the three regional workshops.

The major achievement of the meeting was the enthusiasm and engagement of all participants across the entire week, and their active contribution to the many interactive sessions.

---

[3]United Nations, *Sustainable Development Goal 5: Achieve Gender Equality and Empower All Women and Girls,* https://www.un.org/sustainabledevelopment/gender-equality/.

Figure 11: No longer alone!

Recommendations

The recommendations follow from the findings of the project tasks and discussions held within the network created around the project.

We start with **instructors and parents**, who have an important role to play in changing societal perceptions and stereotypes towards women in science and in engaging girls in primary, secondary, and higher education in the scientific disciplines. We continue with recommendations for **scientific or educational organizations** of all kinds, since these are the places where scientific life takes place daily. We conclude with recommendations for Scientific Unions and other worldwide organizations, in particular the **members of the project**.

For instructors and parents

1.1 Avoid **gender stereotyping and unconscious gender bias** in interactions with female students and children. Adopt practices that encourage girls to participate in scientific activities in schools and non-school settings. Teach boys and girls about gender equity.

1.2 Avoid books and social media that reinforce the gender gap in science. Use books and media **promoting gender balance** and highlighting the contributions of women in science.

1.3 Develop **gender awareness** in the classroom and encourage girls in their learning of scientific subjects. Track who you are engaging in class to ensure that every student has a chance to participate and that girls feel comfortable in speaking up.

1.4 Encourage **relevant single-sex activities** to raise girls' self-confidence and possibilities for expressing themselves.

For local organizations

By local Organizations we mean scientific or educational organizations of all kinds: science departments at universities, conference centres, research groups in industry, etc.

2.1 Promote a **respectful, collegial working atmosphere** in your organization. Monitor support, well-being and mentoring of female academics.

2.2 Define best practices to prevent, report and address **sexual harassment and discrimination** in professional spaces.

2.3 Address the **impact of parenthood** on the careers of women. Introduce proper accounting (18 months per child recommended) for child care responsibilities when evaluating candidates in hiring and promotions processes.[4] In practice, this applies mainly to women. Encourage provision of a research-only year after maternity leave or parental leave. Acknowledge and accept the existence of discontinuous careers and family responsibilities and take these into account in hiring and funding policies.

2.4 Ensure **transparency** of statistics on salaries, course loadings, bonuses, hiring and promotion, observing progress or difficulties experienced by female academics. Encourage policies to help reduce gendered salary disparities. Ensure female and male representation on recruitment committees and provide unconscious bias training for all members. Make the gender lens the responsibility of a dedicated person.

2.5 Welcome families and provide **child friendly environments**. Provide improved support systems for parents. Allocate teaching loads with suitable hours for parents. For conference centres, take care of the issues of families attending with children and equip family rooms in the guest houses to cater for all basic needs (e.g., children's toys, high chairs and changing tables for babies).

2.6 Address **gender equality** in all institutional policies. Identify a person or a group in charge of gender equality inside the organization, looking at the gender balance in all kinds of activities. Put in place initiatives encouraging women. Involve men in identifying barriers and addressing them. Diversity action plans should have financial consequences if not met.

2.7 In all outreach and educational programs, include the **aim of reducing the gender gap**. Adapt such programs to the region or discipline concerned by the organization and evaluate their effectiveness. Develop gender awareness of future teachers and provide training in critical thinking.

---

[4]European Research Council, Working Group on Gender Balance, *Measures and Practices to Improve Gender Balance*,
`https://erc.europa.eu/thematic-working-groups/working-group-gender-balance`.

                                              Results and recommendations

For scientific unions

By Unions we mean worldwide members of the International Science Council, in particular those that are members of our project.

3.1 Work collectively to **change culture and norms** to reduce the various aspects of the gender gap. Share policy, toolkits and learnings to enable member organizations and members. Launch campaigns to increase awareness of the benefits to society of reducing the gender gap.

3.2 Define and advertise **best practices** to prevent, report and address sexual harassement and discrimination in professional spaces.

3.3 In order to address the disproportionate **impact of parenthood** on the careers of women, recommend and disseminate in the scientific community proper accounting of child bearing/caring responsibilities (18 months per child recommended) when evaluating candidates in hiring and promotion processes. Recognise the existence and impact of discontinuous careers and suggest strategies for developing responsive hiring and funding policies. Encourage policies to help reduce salary disparities.

3.4 Actively promote the **visibility of female scientists**, in particular at conferences. Program a session for all participants on diversity and inclusion in their discipline in union-sponsored conferences. Develop policies on gender balance for funding conferences with representative speaker and panel lists, scientific organizing Committees and local organizing committees. Request a reporting mechanism for these concerns at the conference.

3.5 Encourage the **diversification of scientific awards**, actively encouraging the nomination of women. Add 18 months per child to all age-limits in scientific awards for people having taken care of children.

3.6 Encourage the presence of **women in editorial boards** in your discipline and publish reports on the proportion of papers published by women. Use double blind reviews. Manage constructive feedback on submitted papers.

3.7 **Welcome families** in scientific activities. For scientific meetings that you sponsor or support, encourage taking care of all issues of family attending with children and putting a budget in place to offer childcare solutions.

3.8 Create a **committee for women** and/or gender equality, with an assigned budget line. Organize specific meetings to promote women's networking. Support women in writing better grant proposals. Develop websites for women in science, reporting all the news relevant for women in science such as success stories of female scientists, conferences or activities relevant to women in science. Encourage and advertise books and media written by women, biographies of women, and media releases.

3.9 Actively **promote gender balance** at every level of your organization, including its leadership, its committees and also institutional events.

3.10 In all outreach and educational programs and products, **raise awareness** about the gender gap and include specific actions/events that aim at reducing the gender gap. When role models are introduced, include diverse backgrounds, genders and ages, and those who did not necessarily have a straightforward traditional career, including scientists not employed in academia.

Future of the project

Are there plans to keep the Gender Gap in Science Project alive?

All union and organization representatives in the project wish the project results and its associated tools to remain available well beyond the end of the 2017–2019 period during which it received funding from the ISC. Dissemination of our results and coordination towards the implementation of our recommendations is essential. Research questions raised by the tasks of the project are numerous.

The Gender Gap in Science project is eager to participate in the scoping workshop planned by ISC for the "Gender-transformative science" ISC objective. Our minimal plans for the future are the following:

- To use current technology ("data suppression technique") in order to provide access to the data collected through the Global Survey of Scientists to all participating unions and partners of the project, as well as to other research groups upon approval by an ad-hoc committee, while protecting the privacy of the respondents to the survey;

- to organize the long-term availability and maintenance of the tools of the project for the analysis of Publication Patterns and the Data Base of Good Practices.

Depending on the support we find we would also like

- to continue research on the problems identified by the various tasks of the project;

- to organize dissemination activities through workshops in the developing world;

- to organize a coordination meeting every year.

Acknowledgments

Special thanks to Anathea Brooks, Mei-Hung Chiu, Igle Gledhill, Merrilyn Goos, Rachel Ivie, Laura Merner, Helena Mihaljević, Silvina Ponce Dawson, Francesca Primas, Lucia Santamaria Jean Taylor, Jodi Tims and Susan White for their valuable contributions, comments and suggestions for this chapter.

Thanks to all of them, as well as Alice Abreu, Tonya Blowers, Roseanne Diab, Ernesto Fernandez Polcuch, Nathalie Fomproix, Catherine Jami and Regina Kelly for their key contributions to the completion of this project.

References

[1] European Comission, Directorate-General for Employment, Social Affairs and Inclusion (European Commission). *One hundred words for equality. A glossary of terms on equality between women and men*. Luxembourg, LU: Publications Office of the European Union, Oct. 1998. ISBN: 92-828-2627-9.

[2] R. Ivie and C. L. Tesfaye. "Women in physics: A tale of limits." In: *Physics Today* 65.2 (Feb. 2012), pp. 47–50. DOI: 10.1063/PT.3.1439. URL: https://www.aip.org/statistics/reports/global-survey-physicists.

[3] Helena Mihaljević, Marco Tullney, Lucía Santamaría, and Christian Steinfeldt. "Reflections on Gender Analyses of Bibliographic Corpora." In: *Frontiers in Big Data* 2 (2019), p. 29. ISSN: 2624-909X. DOI: 10.3389/fdata.2019.00029. URL: https://www.frontiersin.org/article/10.3389/fdata.2019.00029.

[4] Helena Mihaljević-Brandt, Lucía Santamaría, and Marco Tullney. "The Effect of Gender in the Publication Patterns in Mathematics." In: *PLOS ONE* 11.10 (Oct. 2016), pp. 1–23. DOI: 10.1371/journal.pone.0165367. URL: https://doi.org/10.1371/journal.pone.0165367.

[5] UNESCO. *The SAGA Science, Technology and Innovation Gender Objectives List (STI GOL), SAGA Working paper 1*. Paris, 2016. ISBN: 978-92-3-100154-3. URL: https://unesdoc.unesco.org/ark:/48223/pf0000245006.

Measuring and Analyzing the Gender Gap in Science through the Global Survey of Scientists

Rachel Ivie

Susan White

Measuring and analyzing the gender gap in science through the global survey of scientists

Rachel Ivie[1], Susan White[2]

1 – Senior Director of Education and Research, American Institute of Physics, College Park, MD, US
2 – Interim Director, Statistical Research Center, American Institute of Physics, College Park, MD, US

1 Methodology

The 2018 Global Survey of Mathematical, Natural, and Computing Scientists seeks to develop a broader picture of the status of mathematicians and scientists across the world. The survey instrument was developed by the Gender Gap in Science Project in collaboration with the American Institute of Physics (AIP). Various questions address specific developmental periods in the education and careers of scientists. The UNESCO Institute for Statistics reports that women constitute less than 30% of scientific researchers worldwide, despite women accounting for 50% of the global population. To understand representation of women in STEM fields, it is important to look at three life phases: 1) childhood, 2) early adulthood, and 3) professional life. The Global Survey takes these phases into account by assessing how scientists perceive their early years, university studies, doctoral studies, and careers.

Parts of this chapter will be proposed for publication as a peer-reviewed article, with an extended list of references.

This document explores gender differences by scientific discipline, regions, and level of human development. The disciplines included are Astronomy, Biology, Chemistry, Computer Science, Mathematics, Mathematics – Applied, and Physics. History and Philosophy of Science, although not a mathematical or natural science, is included in some of the analysis because the International Union of History and Philosophy of Science and Technology was a partnering organization. Low response rates prevented including this discipline in all analyses.

We also examined gender differences within regions to look at trends based on geography, not subject matter. We analyzed the data across twelve regions: Africa, Northern America, Caribbean and Central America, South America, West Asia, Central and Southern Asia, Eastern and South-eastern Asia, Northern Europe, Western Europe, Eastern Europe, Southern Europe, and Oceania (see Figure 1, p. 41).

Finally, we examined gender differences within and across human development levels. Development levels were based on the Human Development Index (HDI) created by the United Nations Development Programme. The index is a composite score that considers health, education, and standard of living in a country.[1] Based on this list, we divided the countries into two categories of development: more developed and less developed. Taiwan is the only country in the survey not included in the UN list. Based on available data on Taiwan's health, education and standard of living, Taiwan was included in the more developed category.

1.1 Survey Design

Goals, priorities, and research questions for the survey were discussed at the launch meeting of the project in June, 2017 in Paris. The overall research questions are: to better understand scientists' development of interest in science, experiences in education and careers, work-life balance, family support, demographics, access to resources needed to conduct science, and opportunities to contribute to the scientific enterprise. The research questions also included the need to make comparisons across regions, disciplines, and level of human development. Using these goals, AIP drafted a questionnaire based largely on

---

[1]United Nations Development Programme, *United Nations Human Development Index*, http://hdr.undp.org/en/content/human-development-index-hdi.

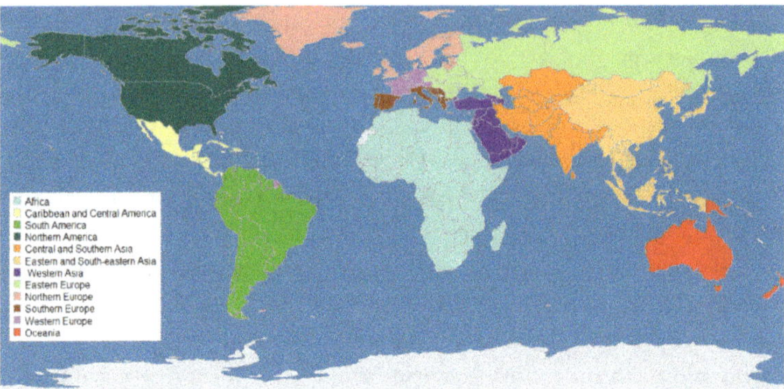

Figure 1: Geographic regions used in the analyses

the previously used Global Survey of Physicists[2] and the UNESCO SAGA questionnaire [6]. AIP reviewed each drafted question to ensure that it 1) met the goals agreed upon at the Paris meeting, 2) contributed significantly to findings, and 3) answered the research questions.

AIP created a draft survey to present at regional meetings held in Colombia, Taiwan, and South Africa. Representatives in these meetings reviewed and provided feedback on the initial draft, including 1) reviewing specific questions to collect feedback on regional implications of wording and topics, 2) input on the full survey instrument with special consideration to ensure that the questions work for the region and for all disciplines, and 3) an outline of the distribution plan. Feedback and comments from each of the meetings were recorded, compiled, and reviewed to edit and update the questionnaire. The edited questionnaire was presented back to the project's executive committee for final approval. After final approval the questionnaire was translated and placed online for distribution.

1.2 Questionnaire Translation

After the executive committee approved the final version of the questionnaire, it was sent to a translation company that specializes in translating questionnaires. The professional

---

[2]For more on the 2009 IUPAP Global Survey of Physicists, see [3, 4].

translation company utilized a three-step process with native speakers of each language. It involves initial translation, followed by a second editing by a second linguist, and finally proofreading by a third linguist. The professional translations were reviewed by project participants to ensure that the translations met the needs of scientists. The reviews by project participants were used to inform the professional translators and refine the translations for the project audience. The questionnaire was translated into Spanish, Russian, French, Chinese, Japanese, and Arabic. The languages were chosen based on input from the participants at the workshops, recommendations from the UN, and on the languages used for IUPAP's Global Survey of Physicists in 2009.

1.3 Sampling

We collected data using a snowball sampling method and contact databases from partnering organizations to reach students and professional scientists across the globe. Since there is not a single network or resource available to contact all students and professional scientists globally, we used snowball sampling to take advantage of as many personal networks as possible.

Snowball sampling is a non-probability method for data collection and does not result in a statistically representative sample. Because of this, there are important limitations of analysis and interpretation for the data collected by the survey. The findings presented in this report should not be assumed to be representative of the intended population as a whole. Therefore, the findings below only indicate trends for the individuals who responded to the survey, not the overall population.

1.4 Data Processing

Primary data collection ended on December 31, 2018. AIP cleaned and prepared the data by finding and solving inconsistencies, creating new variables for analysis, and labeling variables and responses, thereby increasing the quality of the dataset. The process consisted of three steps, (1) data cleaning, (2) translation of open-ended responses, and (3) product preparation. Data cleaning involved processes designed to increase data quality and ensure the accuracy of analyses. We examined each variable individually and through valid groupings of variables to ensure consistency and believability of responses. Skip patterns were logged to allow for a review of the total number of respondents answering each question. Respondents with potential issues were also investigated. For translation, the open-ended responses for each question were linked to the unique identifier for each respondent in order to be able to pair the translated text with a respondent's other answers. There were approximately 250,000 individual words that required translation. Translation was conducted by a professional translation service.

1.5 Analysis Methods

We initially conducted bivariate analyses to provide a simple view of the data. However, bivariate analyses can be confounded by intervening factors, leading to incorrect interpretations.[3] For the final report, we focus on multivariate analyses. The multivariate analyses allow the inclusion of potential confounding factors, such as employment sector, discipline, geographic region, age and more in the analysis. We are still able to test for statistically significant differences in the responses of men and women after accounting for potential confounding factors. In this final report, we focus solely on the multivariate analyses to avoid the possibility of incorrect interpretations resulting from confounding. We have included the graphs of bivariate results where they are consistent with the multivariate results. However, in almost every case, the bivariate analysis understates the relative ratio of men's and women's responses.

Logistic and Ordinal Logistic Regression

We use logistic and ordinal logistic regression analyses [2] to examine gender difference by discipline, by region, and by level of economic development.

In cases where the variable of interest is binary (as in yes/no), we use logistic regression. In this model, we are estimating the log-odds of the event that the variable of interest = 1 (and not 0). We assume a linear relationship of the form:

$$l = \log_b \frac{p}{1-p} = \beta_0 + \beta_1 x_1 + \beta_2 x_2 + \ldots + \beta_k x_k + e,$$

---

[3] For example, we see this confounding effect in the analyses of doctoral program quality ranking. The bivariate analyses did not indicate any gender differences; however, the multivariate analysis reveals that men are likely to rate their doctoral program quality higher than women.

where l is the log-odds, b is the base of the logarithm, β_i are the parameters of the model on the independent variables x_i, e represents random error, and p is the probability that the value of interest is 1 (and not 0).

After the application of algebraic manipulation techniques, this resolves to our final model

$$p = \frac{1}{1 + b^{-(\beta_0 + \beta_1 x_1 + \beta_2 x_2 + \ldots + \beta_k x_k)}}.$$

In the case of a binary dependent variable, we can use the output of the analysis to express the relative likelihood of one event over another. We do so in the tables.

In cases where the variable of interest has multiple options (for example, level of agreement), we use a modified version of this technique called ordinal logistic regression. In these models, the relative likelihood of an event depends on the number of steps of change in the response. For example, a movement from disagree to strongly agree would be three steps in the case of a five-point scale with a neutral point in the middle. Likewise, a change in the response from strongly disagree to agree would also be three steps. So, it is not as straightforward to report a relative likelihood of one response over another. In these cases, we report only the direction of the change, not a relative likelihood.

In all cases, we indicate the independent variables included in the model.

Type I and Type II errors

Due to the sheer number of analyses being run, the likelihood of making a Type I error is increased.[4] We mitigate the number of Type I errors using the Bonferroni correction to compute a lower threshold for statistical significance.[5] In order to be as conservative as possible, we set α lower.[6] We identified the largest number of questions that could be classified as a family (22) and used this to calculate a family-wise error correction: $0.05/22 = 0.002$. Using a lower α increases the probability of making a Type II error.[7] Thus, we consider

---

[4]A Type I error is incorrectly rejecting a true null hypothesis; for more information on Type I errors in statistical hypothesis testing, see [1].

[5]For more information on the Bonferroni correction, see [5].

[6]α is set for a hypothesis test as the threshold for making a Type I error.

[7]A Type II error is failing to reject a false null hypothesis, thinking there is no difference when there really is; for more information on Type II errors in statistical hypothesis testing, see [1].

there to be sufficient evidence to suggest a statistically significant difference if the p-value for the test statistic is < 0.002.

We focus on multivariate analyses because they do account for confounding factors. Thus, differences in a multivariate model cannot be explained by factors in the model. That is, if we see a statistically significant difference between the responses of men and women in a multivariate model that includes discipline, geographic region, country development level, and employment sector, then we believe that the difference in the men's and women's responses is due to gender and not to any other factors. We ran a series of binary logistic and ordinal logistic regressions with the variable of interest as the dependent variable and the following included as independent (explanatory) variables: gender, age (as a proxy for career progress), discipline, employment sector, geographic region, and level of development.

The types of logistic regressions differ because many of our dependent variables are binary (for example, Yes/No). Some are ordinal, (for example, Strongly agree / Agree / Neutral / Disagree / Strongly Disagree), and for these, we combined Strongly agree and Agree into "agree"; we did the same thing with "disagree." Thus, we have: agree / neutral / disagree.

The regression coefficients can be interpreted to tell us whether one group is more (or less) likely than another group to respond in a particular way while accounting for potential confounding factors. So, we can test for differences between women's and men's responses to a question while accounting for potential confounding factors (age, discipline, employment sector, geographic region, and level of development). Similarly, we can test for differences across disciplines while accounting for potential confounding factors (gender, age, employment sector, geographic region, and level of development).

2 Tools Produced

The questionnaire is available online at:

```
https://statisticalresearchcenter.aip.org/global18.
```

3 Results

There were 32,346 respondents to the first question:

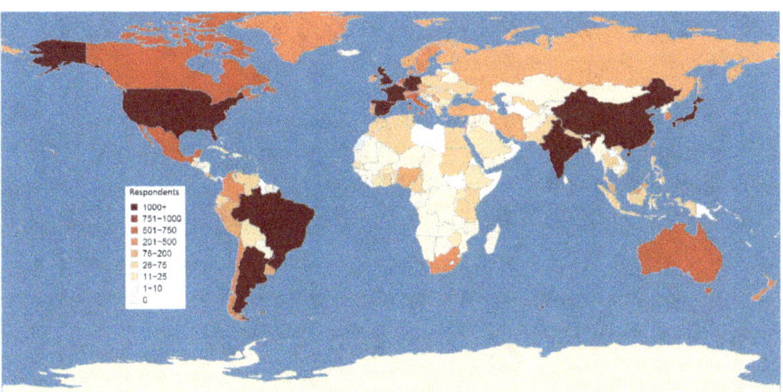

Figure 2: Number of respondents by country.

Table 1: Proportion of women and men among respondents by discipline.

Discipline	Women (%)	Men (%)	n
Astronomy	48	52	2597
Biology	69	31	2960
Chemistry	51	49	2698
Computer Science	55	45	3150
History and Philosophy of Science	46	54	324
Mathematics	43	57	3458
Mathematics – Applied	54	46	2146
Physics	37	63	7570
Overall	**50**	**50**	—

The overall total does not match the 32,346 respondents to question 1 because there are respondents in other disciplines and not every respondent answered the question about their gender. In addition, a respondent could have a university degree in one discipline and be employed in a different discipline. Thus, these numbers are different at different stages in the questionnaire. The data above reflect the discipline corresponding to "primary field of study."

*"Have you studied or worked in mathematical, computing or natural sciences,
or in the history and philosophy of science and technology?"*

The number of responses to subsequent questions varied based on skip patterns and respondent participation. We collected data from 159 unique countries, although the number of respondents from each varied (Figure 2, p. 46).

Women and men are almost equally represented in the overall data set. Three hundred and eighty respondents preferred not to respond to the question querying their gender, and, therefore, their responses are not included in these analyses, which focus on differences in experiences between women and men. In Table 1 (p. 46), we provide a breakdown of

Table 2: Proportion of women and men among respondents by geographic region.

Geographic Region	Woman (%)	Men (%)	n
Africa	61	39	1265
Northern America	56	44	5003
Caribbean and Central America	52	48	664
South America	53	47	3314
Western Asia	59	41	395
Central and Southern Asia	45	55	1416
Eastern and South-eastern Asia	36	64	4655
Northern Europe	58	42	2097
Western Europe	46	54	7639
Eastern Europe	47	53	574
Southern Europe	53	47	2039
Oceania	60	40	927
Overall	**50**	**50**	—

The overall total does not match the 32,346 respondents to question 1 because not every respondent answered the question about their gender. In addition, a respondent could have graduated from secondary school in one geographic region, earned their first university degree in a second, earned a second university degree in another, and be primarily employed in yet another. Thus, these numbers vary at different stages in the questionnaire. The data above are for the respondents' current location.

the proportion of men and women among respondents by discipline. In Table 2 (p. 47), we provide a breakdown of the proportion of men and women among respondents by geographic region.

3.1 Multivariate Analysis: Sexual Harassment

We first turn to the issue of harassment. We asked a question: Have you ever encountered sexual harassment at school or work? We compare the respondents who replied *"yes, it happened to me"* with those who did not reply that *"it happened to me."* We first ran a model with all respondents with gender, age, discipline, employment sector, geographic region, and Human Development Index as independent variables.

Results from this model allow us to compare the experiences of men and women while accounting for age, discipline, employment sector, geographic region, and level of human development. The results indicate that women are 14.4 times more likely to indicate having personally experienced sexual harassment at school or work than men – 1440% more likely.

We then examined the experience of women in each discipline separately using gender, age, employment sector, geographic region, and HDI as independent variables.

The results are shown graphically in Figure 3 (p. 49). In short, women in every discipline were more likely to indicate having personally experienced sexual harassment at school or work than men. Given the standard error in the estimates, we can say there is no one discipline in which the likelihood is lower for women than any other discipline.

While these results are consistent with the observations in the bivariate analyses (Figure 4, p. 50), the raw data from Figure 4 (p. 50) *understates* the relative likelihood for women, compared to men, to have experienced sexual harassment at school or work after taking into account confounding factors such as age, geographic region, employment sector, and level of development.

The data in Figure 3 (p. 49) should be used to measure or quantify the relative likelihood for women compared to men. For example, according to Figure 3 (p. 49), a woman in astronomy is about 20 times more likely to encounter sexual harassment at school or work than a man. Yet, the raw data (Figure 4, p. 50) shown in the bivariate (30% for women versus 3% for men) *understates* relative likelihood in astronomy. Furthermore, the relative value in Figure 4, p. 50 (30%/3% = 10 times more likely) is below the lower point of the interval estimated based on the multivariate model.

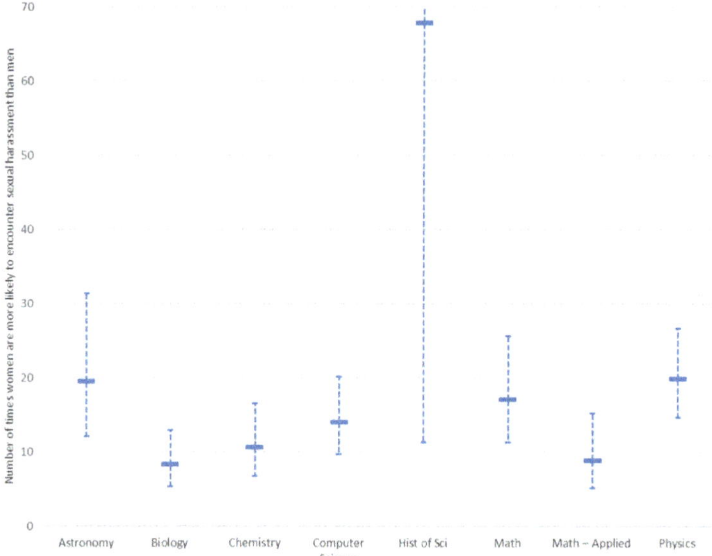

The horizontal bar indicates the point estimate, and the dashed lines indicate the standard error. The standard error is much larger for History of Science due to a smaller number of respondents.

Figure 3: Encountering sexual harassment at school or work by discipline.

We also examined the experience of women in each geographic region separately using gender, age, discipline, employment sector, and HDI as independent variables.

The results are shown graphically in Figure 5 (p. 51). In short, women in every geographic region were more likely to indicate having personally experienced sexual harassment at school or work than men, except for Western Asia. This means that there was no statistical difference between men and women in Western Asia. Given the standard error in the estimates, we can say there is no one geographic region in which the likelihood is lower for women than any other geographic region. Again, this is consistent with the bivariate findings (Figure 6, p. 52), but the bivariate image *understates* the relative likelihood in most cases.

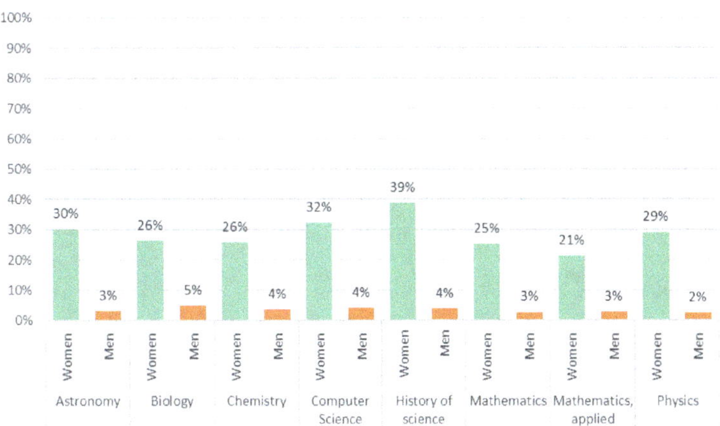

Each of these statistically significant relative differences (30% to 3%, or 10 times, in Astronomy, for example) *understates* the relative likelihood between women and men in the multivariate model which accounts for confounding factors including age, geographic region, employment sector, and level of development.

Figure 4:   Respondents indicating they personally encountered sexual harassment at school or work by discipline.

We also examined the experience of women by *level of development*[8] separately using gender, age, discipline, employment sector, and geographic region as independent variables.

The results are shown graphically in Figure 7 (p. 53). In short, women in both HDI groups were more likely to indicate having personally experienced sexual harassment at school or work than men, Given the standard error in the estimates, we can say there is no difference in the likelihood for women by HDI. Again, this is consistent with the findings in the bivariate analysis (see Figure 8, p. 54).

Finally, we examined the experience of women in different employment sectors separately using gender, age, discipline, geographic region, and HDI as independent variables.

The results are shown graphically in Figure 9 (p. 55). In short, women in every employment sector were more likely to indicate having personally experienced sexual harassment at

---

[8]Higher development includes countries with an HDI 0.700 or greater; lower development includes those with and HDI < 0.700.

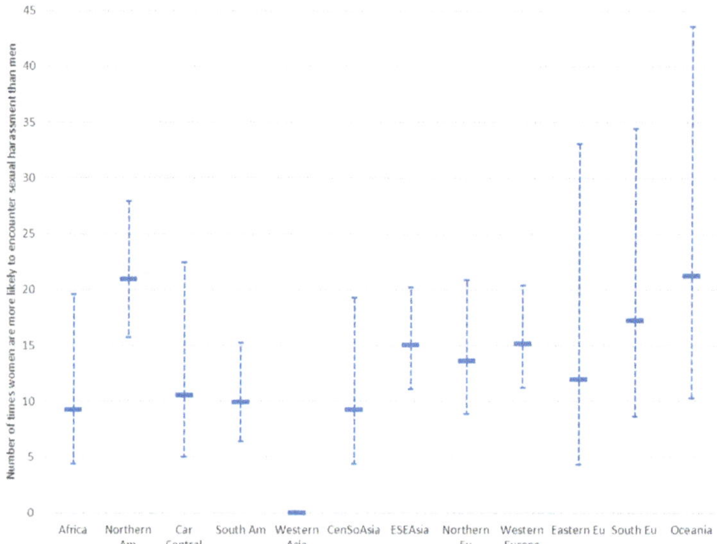

The horizontal bar indicates the point estimate, and the dashed lines indicate the standard error. The size of the standard error depends on the number of respondents.

Figure 5: Encountering sexual harassment at school or work by geographic region.

school or work than men. Given the standard error in the estimates, we can say there is no employment sector in which the likelihood is lower for women than any other employment sector.

The statistical models are not the only source of information. We have begun conducting qualitative analysis on some open-ended questions. One respondent reported:

> *"My institution does not have a defined sexual harassment policy. I reported a supervisor for sexual harassment and had a terrible experience during the HR investigation."*

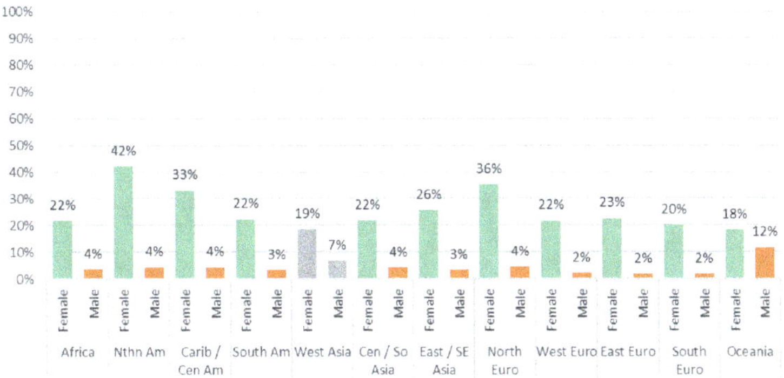

Each of these statistically significant relative differences (22% to 4%, or 5.5 times, in Africa, for example) *understates* the relative likelihood between women and men in the multivariate model which accounts for confounding factors including age, discipline, employment sector, and level of development.

The gray bars indicate that the difference is not statistically significant at the 0.002 level.

Figure 6: Percentages of respondents indicating they personally encountered sexual harassment at school or work by geographic region.

3.2 Multivariate Analysis: Gender Differences in Educational Experiences

We now consider respondents' educational experiences. We turn now to the multivariate analysis, which can account for confounding factors that the bivariate analysis cannot reveal. We ran logistic regressions for sixteen questions from the survey:

- *Choose field.* When did you choose your primary field of study?
- Who encouraged you in your studies?
    - *Encourage: Partner.* Spouse or partner
    - *Encourage: Parents.* Parents
    - *Encourage: Other family.* Other family members
    - *Encourage: Employ/colleagues.* Employer or colleagues
    - *Encourage: Community.* Your neighborhood, community, or friends
    - *Encourage: Teachers/Profs/Mentors.* Teachers, professors, or mentors

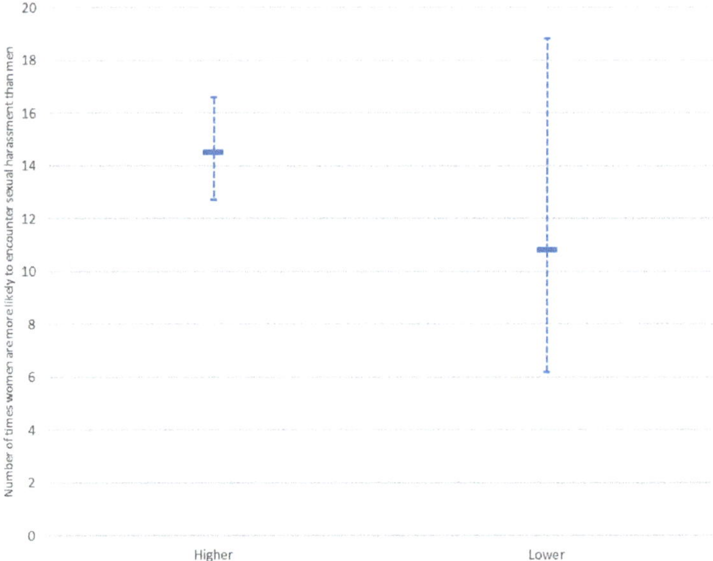

The horizontal bar indicates the point estimate, and the dashed lines indicate the standard error. The size of the standard error depends on the number of respondents.

Figure 7: Encountering sexual harassment at school or work by level of development.

>   — *Encourage: Other students.* Other students
>
>   — *Encourage: Own determination.* Your own determination, will power, and hard work

- *Doctoral program quality.* How would you rate the quality of your doctoral program?

- *Doctoral advisor support.* In my doctoral experience, I had support from my advisor or supervisor.

- *Doctoral program fair treatment.* In my doctoral experience, my program treated everyone fairly.

- *Interruptions in doctoral studies.* Have there been any significant interruptions in your doctoral studies?

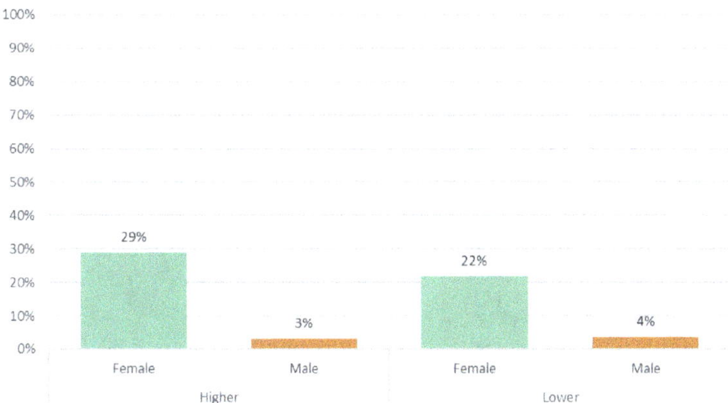

Both of these statistically significant relative differences 29% to 3%, or ~ 10 times, in countries with higher development levels, for example) *understate* the relative likelihood between women and men in the multivariate model which accounts for confounding factors including age, discipline, employment sector, and geographic region.

Figure 8: Percentages of respondents indicating they personally encountered sexual harassment at school or work by level of human development.

We ran multivariate models for each of these twelve questions using gender, age, discipline, geographic region, and HDI as independent variables. Note that we do not include employment sector because the variables of interest are about educational experiences. The results are shown in Table 3 (p. 56).

Overall, we find no statistically significant gender differences in the timing of choosing one's discipline. Women are more likely to report that their families encouraged them in their studies than men, and women are more likely than men to report being encouraged by their own determination, will power, and hard work. There are no statistically significant differences in the responses of men and women regarding other sources of encouragement. Men are more likely to report positive experiences in their doctoral programs, and women are more likely to report interruptions in their doctoral programs. One woman who responded told us,

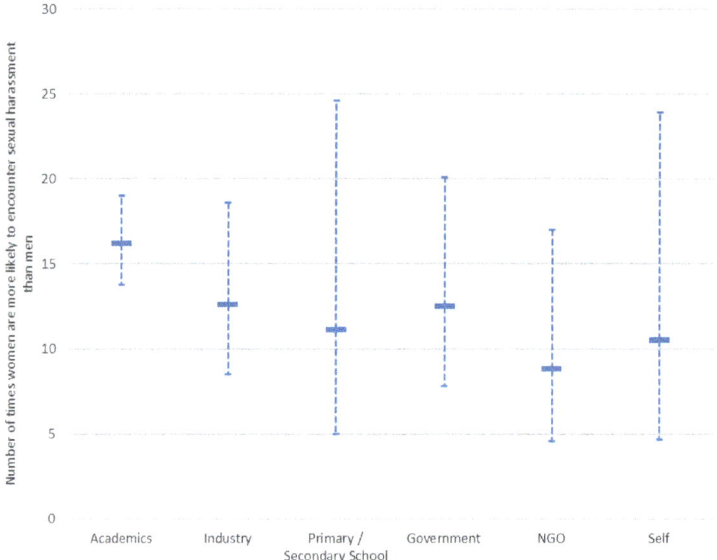

The horizontal bar indicates the point estimate, and the dashed lines indicate the standard error. The size of the standard error depends on the number of respondents.

Figure 9: Encountering sexual harassment at school or work by employment sector.

> *"Unconditional support from my family and the available resources form my parents"*

had helped her succeed. Another attributed her success to

> *"being stubborn and unwilling to let the bad guys win!!!"*

On the other hand, another respondent told us about her thesis advisor:

> *"Harassment (psychological) by my thesis director, which was persistent, and people knew about it in the laboratory, but [I did not receive] any support for fear of reprisals."*

These echo the findings above.

A Closer Look at Gender Differences in Educational Experiences by Discipline

In order to better understand gender differences by discipline, we ran a multivariate model for each discipline separately. That allows us to look at gender differences within a specific discipline. We examine some of those findings below. We find that there is a statistically significant difference in the timing for men and women whose primary field is computer science or mathematics – applied (see Figure 10, p. 57).

We also find that there is a statistically significant difference in the rating of doctoral program quality for men and women whose primary field is astronomy, chemistry, math-

Table 3: Gender differences in educational experiences.

Item	Gender Differences
Choose field	No statistically significant gender differences.
Encourage: Partner	**Women 1.7 times more likely** to say **spouse or partner** than men.
Encourage: Parents	**Women 1.4 times more likely** to say **parents** than men.
Encourage: Other family	**Women 1.2 times more likely** to say **other family members** than men.
Encourage: Employ / colleagues	No statistically significant gender differences.
Encourage: Community	No statistically significant gender differences.
Encourage: Teachers / profs / mentors	No statistically significant gender differences.
Encourage: Other students	No statistically significant gender differences.
Encourage: Own determination	**Women 1.1 times more likely** to say **own determination** than men.
Doctoral program quality[†]	**Men likely** to rate quality **higher** than women.
Doctoral advisor support[†]	**Men likely** to rate advisor support **better** than women.
Doctoral program fair treatment[†]	**Men likely** to **agree more strongly** than women.
Interruptions in doctoral studies	**Women 1.6 times more likely** to say **Yes** than men.

These gender differences are statistically significant at the $\alpha = 0.002$ level after accounting for potential confounding factors (age, discipline, geographic region, and level of development).

[†] The dependent variable is ordinal, so we are unable to report a single odds ratio.

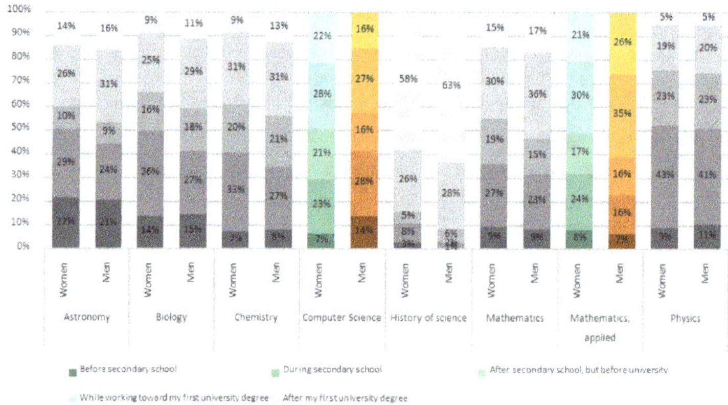

Gray indicates the differences are not statistically significant by gender at the 0.002 level.

Figure 10: Percentages of respondents indicating the period of time they chose their primary field by discipline.

ematics, or physics (see Figure 11, p. 58). We see a similar pattern for the respondents indicating they had a positive relationship with their advisor or supervisor during doctoral studies (see Figure 12, p. 58).

We also see statistically significant differences in respondents' opinion of fair treatment in their doctoral program by gender (Figure 13, p. 59) and in respondents indicating they had a significant interruption in their doctoral studies by discipline (Figure 14, p. 59).

A Closer Look at Gender Differences in Educational Experiences by Geographic Region

As we did with each of the disciplines, we ran a multivariate model for each geographic region separately. We examine some of those findings below. We find that there is a statistically significant difference in the proportion of respondents indicating they had a positive relationship with their advisor or supervisor during doctoral studies (see Figure 15, p. 60).

We also find that there is a statistically significant difference in the rating of fair treatment in the doctoral program for men and women who studied in several regions (see Figure 16,

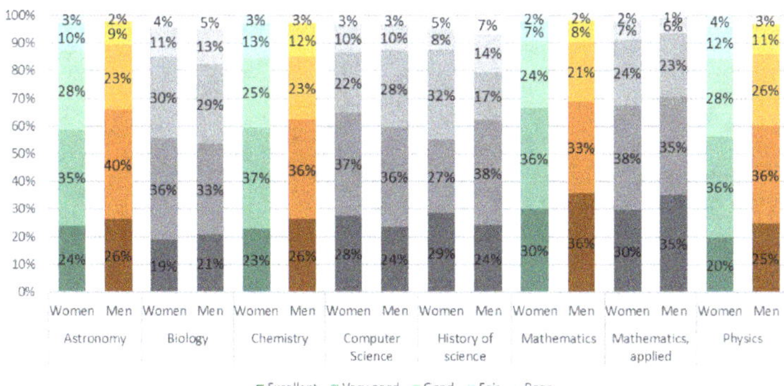

Gray indicates the differences are not statistically significant by gender at the 0.002 level.

Figure 11: Percentages of respondents' rating of quality of doctoral program by discipline.

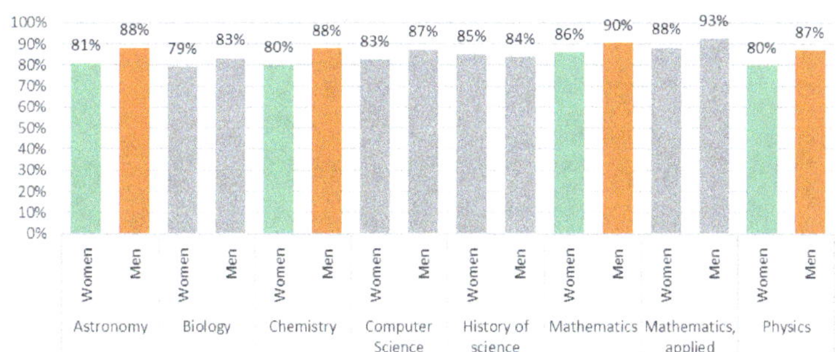

Gray indicates the differences are not statistically significant by gender at the 0.002 level.

Figure 12: Percentages of respondents indicating they had a positive relationship with their advisor or supervisor during doctoral studies by discipline.

p. 60). Figure 17 (p. 61) depicts gender differences in interruptions in doctoral programs by geographic region.

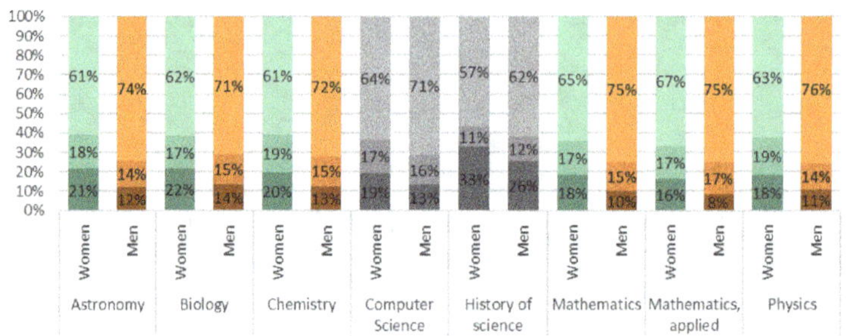

Gray indicates the differences are not statistically significant by gender at the 0.002 level.

Figure 13: Percentages of sespondents' agreement with the statement, *"My program treated every-one fairly"* by discipline.

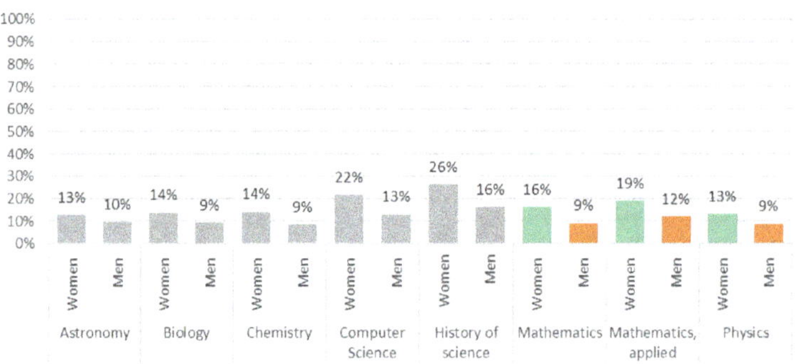

Each of these statistically significant relative differences (16% for women to 9% for men, or ~ 1.8 times, in Mathematics, for example) *understates* the relative likelihood between women and men in the multivariate model which accounts for confounding factors including age, employment sector, geographic region, and level of development.

Gray indicates the differences are not statistically significant by gender at the 0.002 level.

Figure 14: Percentages of respondents indicating they had significant interruptions in their doctoral studies by discipline.

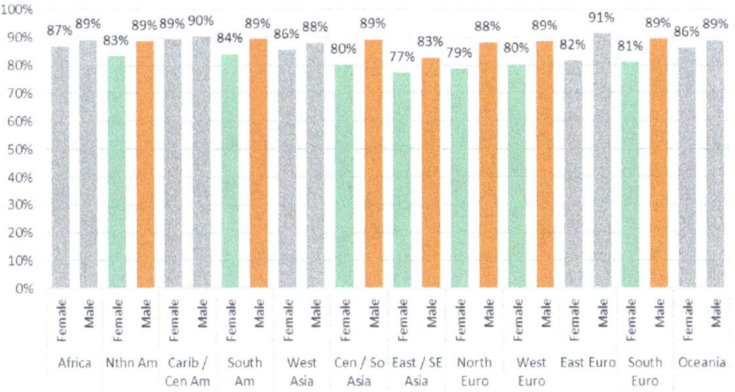

Gray indicates the differences are not statistically significant by gender at the 0.002 level.

Figure 15: Percentages of respondents indicating they had a positive relationship with their advisor or supervisor during doctoral studies by geographic region.

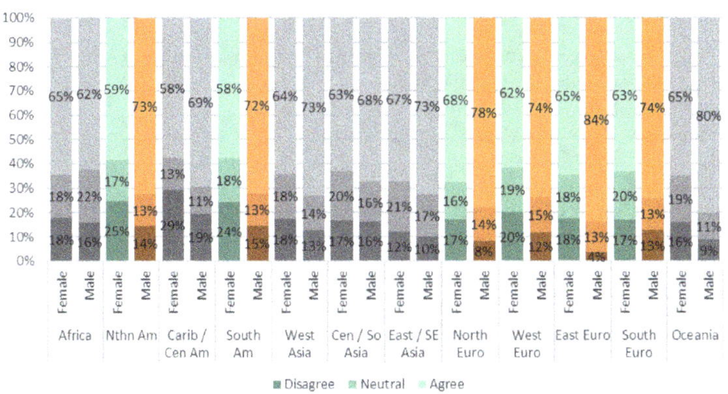

Gray indicates the differences are not statistically significant by gender at the 0.002 level.

Figure 16: Percentages of respondents agreement with the statement, *"My program treated everyone fairly"* by geographic region.

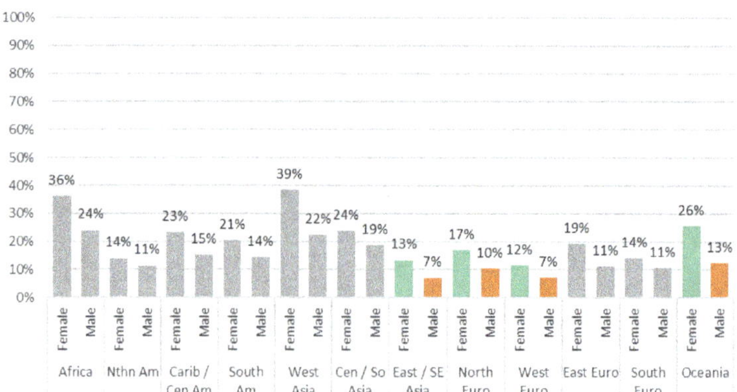

Each of thesestatistically significant relative differences (13% for women to 7% for men, or ~ 1.9 times, in East / SE Asia, for example) *understates* the relative likelihood between women and men in the multivariate model which accounts for confounding factors including age, employment sector, discipline, and level of development.

Gray indicates the differences are not statistically significant by gender at the 0.002 level.

Figure 17: Percentages of respondents indicating they had significant interruptions in their doctoral studies by geographic region.

A Closer Look at Gender Differences in Educational Experiences by Level of Development

As we did with discipline and geographic region, we ran separate multivariate models for countries with higher and lower levels of economic development. We examine some of those findings below. We find that there is no statistically significant difference in the ratings of doctoral program quality by level of development. We do see a statistically significant difference in the proportion of respondents indicating they had a positive relationship with their advisor or supervisor during doctoral studies in countries with higher levels of development, but not in those with a lower level of development (see Figure 18, p. 62).

We also find that there is a statistically significant difference in the rating of fair treatment in the doctoral program for men and women whose primary field in several countries with

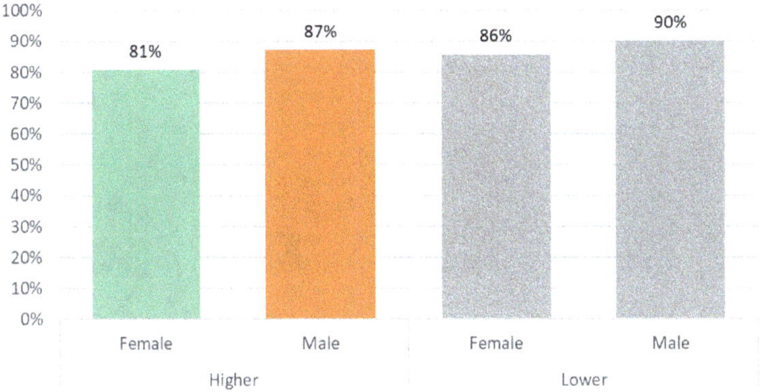

Gray indicates the differences are not statistically significant by gender at the 0.002 level.

Figure 18: Percentages of respondents indicating they had a positive relationship with their advisor or supervisor during doctoral studies by level of development.

higher levels of economic development (see Figure 19, p. 63). Figure 20 (p. 64) depicts gender differences in interruptions in doctoral programs by level of development.

3.3 Multivariate Analysis: Gender Differences in Employment Experiences

We have seen that there are gender differences in educational experiences. We next tested for any gender differences in employment experiences. As before, we ran a series of multivariate regression models examining responses to the following questions:

- *Employer fair treatment.* At my current job, my employer treats everyone fairly.

- *Respectful co-workers.* My co-workers are respectful of everyone.

- *Rate of career progression.* Compared to colleagues who completed their final degrees at the same time as you, how quickly have you progressed in your career?

Our multivariate models used gender, age, discipline, employment sector, geographic region, and HDI as independent variables. The results are shown in Table 4 (p. 63).

In each of these items, men reported more positive experiences than women. One noted:

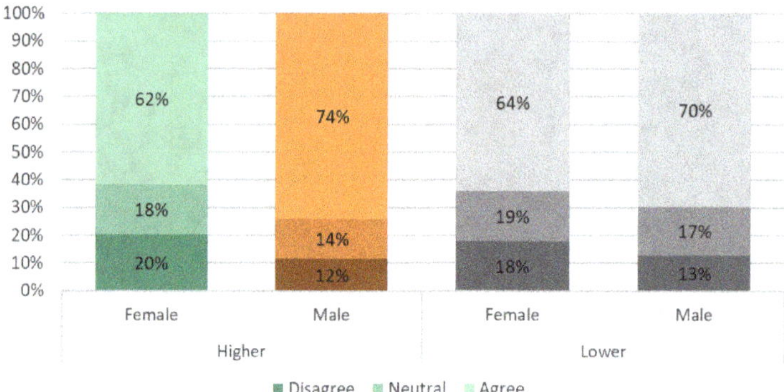

Gray indicates the differences are not statistically significant by gender at the 0.002 level.

Figure 19: Percentages of respondents' agreement with the statement, *"My program treated everyone fairly"* by level of development.

"Sexism is constant and prevalent everywhere, and it's exhausting."

In some situations, women feel isolated in addition to facing the more negative experiences. One respondent wrote:

"Working in a fully male environment, I sometimes feel there is no one to talk to."

Table 4: Gender differences in employment experiences.

Item	Gender Differences
Employer fair treatment[†]	**Men likely** to **agree more strongly** than women.
Respectful co-workers[†]	**Men likely** to **agree more strongly** than women.
Rate of career progression[†]	**Men likely** to report **faster career progression** than women.

These gender differences are statistically significant at the $\alpha = 0.002$ level after accounting for potential confounding factors (age, discipline, geographic region, and level of development).

[†] The dependent variable is ordinal, so we are unable to report a single odds ratio.

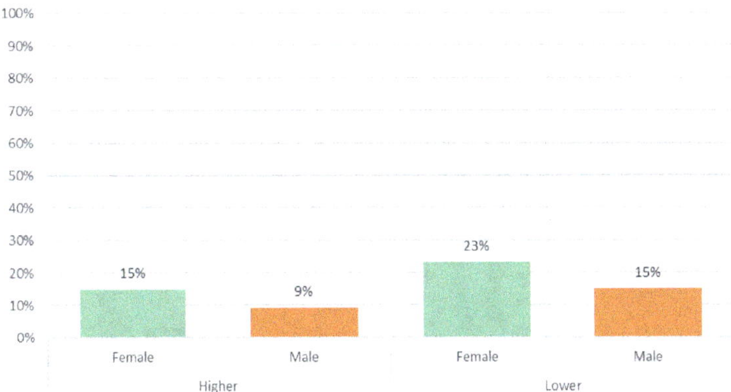

Both of these relative differences (15% for men to 9% for women, or ∼ 1.7 times, in countries with higher development levels, for example) *understate* the relative likelihood between women and men in the multivariate model which accounts for confounding factors including age, employment sector, discipline, and geographic region.

Figure 20: Percentages of respondents indicating they had significant interruptions in their doctoral studies by level of development.

Even when other women are present, women can still feel excluded. Another respondent said:

> *"There are few women in my department, and for the first three years I almost always ate lunch alone. Only the men arrange to eat lunch as a group, and they rarely invite me."*

A Closer Look at Gender Differences in Employment Experiences by Discipline

As before, we ran a multivariate model for each discipline separately to look at gender differences within a specific discipline. We examine some of those findings below. We find that there is a statistically significant difference men's and women's agreement with the statement, *"My employer treats everyone fairly."* (see Figure 21, p. 65).

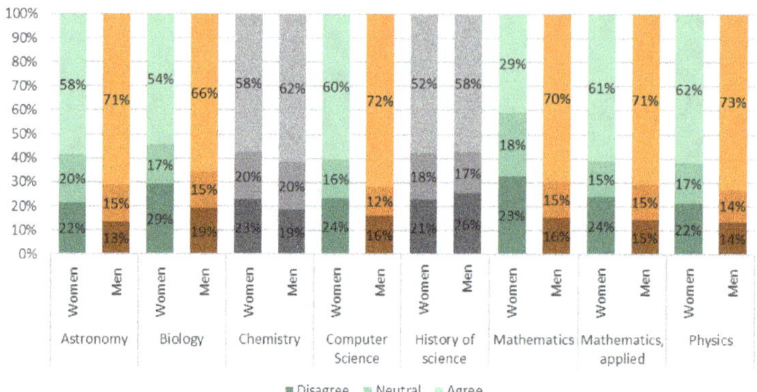

Gray indicates the differences are not statistically significant by gender at the 0.002 level.

Figure 21: Percentages of respondents' agreement with the statement, *"My employer treats everyone fairly"* by discipline.

We also find that there is a statistically significant difference in respondents' career progression by discipline (see Figure 22, p. 66).

A Closer Look at Gender Differences in Employment Experiences by Geographic Region

As before, we ran multivariate models for each geographic region in order to better understand gender differences in employment experiences in the different regions. We examine some of those findings below. We find that there is a statistically significant difference in the proportion of respondents indicating their employer treats every fairly (see Figure 23, p. 66).

In regions other than Africa, Caribbean / Central America, and West Asia, men and women had statistically significant difference in their agreement with the statement, *"My co-workers are respectful of everyone."* (see Figure 24, p. 67).

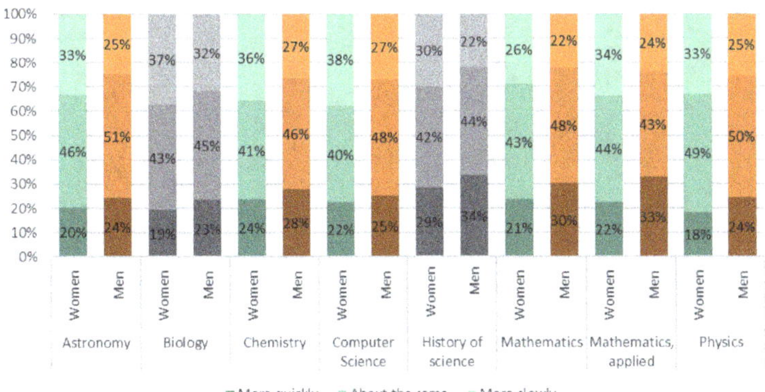

Gray indicates the differences are not statistically significant by gender at the 0.002 level.

Figure 22: Percentages of respondents comparing their career progression to their colleagues who completed their final degrees at the same time by discipline.

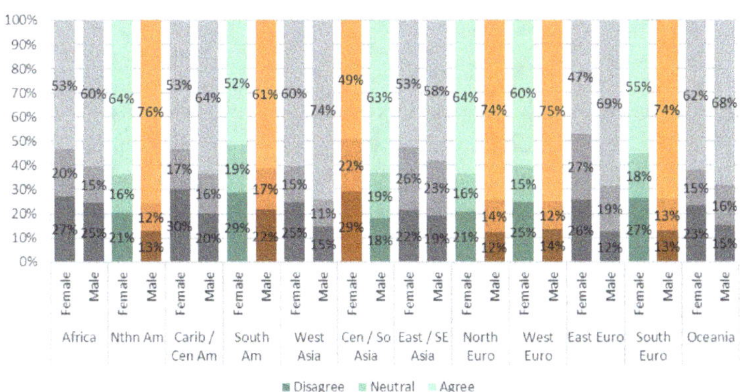

Gray indicates the differences are not statistically significant by gender at the 0.002 level.

Figure 23: Percentages of respondents agreement with the statement, *"My employer treats everyone fairly"* by geographic region.

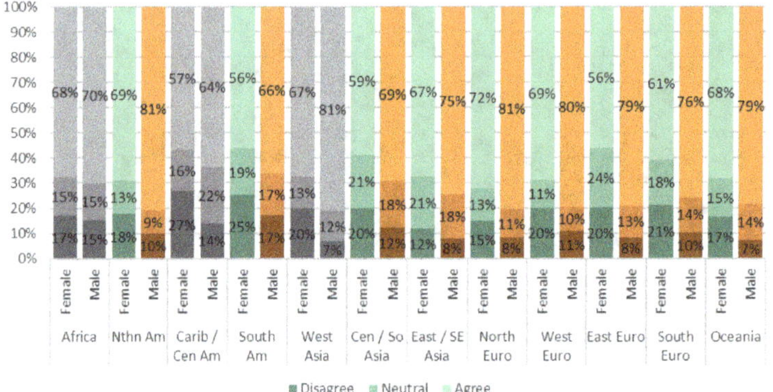

Gray indicates the differences are not statistically significant by gender at the 0.002 level.

Figure 24: Percentages of respondents agreement with the statement, *"My co-workers are respectful of everyone"* by geographic region.

A Closer Look at Gender Differences in Employment Experiences by Level of Development

Again, we ran two multivariate models for countries that with higher and lower levels of economic development to look at gender differences by level of development. We find respondents' agreement with the statement, *"My employer treats everyone fairly,"* is statistically significant difference in both countries with higher and lower levels of development (see Figure 25, p. 68). We see the same pattern with respondents' agreement with the statement, *"My co-workers are respectful of everyone."* (see Figure 26, p. 68).

3.4 Multivariate Analysis: Gender Differences in Access to Resources and Opportunities

We asked questions about respondents' access to resources needed to conduct science and to opportunities to participate in the scientific enterprise. For resources, we asked respondents whether they had *"enough of the following to conduct or present [their] research."*

- Funding

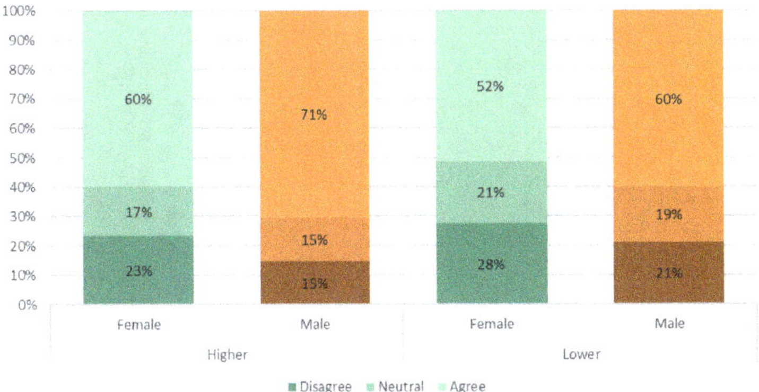

Figure 25: Percentages of respondents' agreement with the statement, *"My employer treats every-one fairly"* by level of development.

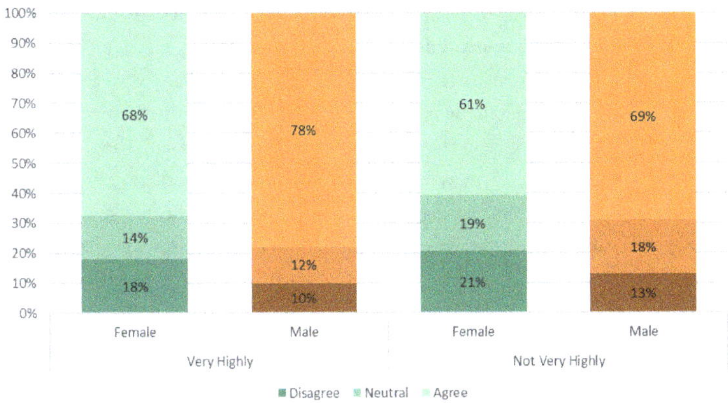

Figure 26: Percentages of respondents' agreement with the statement, *"My co-workers are respect-ful of everyone"* by level of development.

- Office space

- Lab space

- Equipment

- Travel money

- Clerical support

- Employees or students

- Computing capability

- Technical support

- Access to data

- Access to scientific literature

- Support as a working parent

For this analysis of twelve different resources, we summed the number of items for which the respondent indicated *"yes."* Overall, the mean number of resources available to respondents was 7.4 (median = 8). There is a statistically significant difference in the total number of resources available to men (7.6) and women (7.2). However, some of this gender difference might be attributable to differences in discipline, employment sector, geographic region, HDI, or a respondent's age. We ran a multivariate regression to see whether the statistically significant difference in means could be explained by other factors. However, the difference seen in the regression model is virtually the same with men having, on average, 0.4 more resources available than women. While the difference is small, the effect can have a cumulative effect on careers, placing men at a potential advantage compared to women.

For opportunities, we asked respondents whether they had participated in the following:

- Given a talk at a conference as an invited speaker;

- Attended a conference abroad;

- Conducted research abroad;

- Acted as a boss or manager;

- Served as editor of a journal;

- Served on committees for grant agencies;

- Served on important committees at your institute or company;

- Served on an organizing committee for a conference in your field;

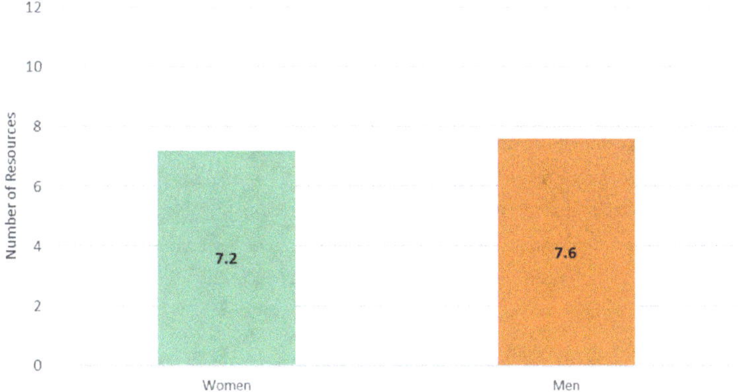

This represents access to resources in one year. This difference can compound though one's career.

Figure 27: Average number of resources available to men and women.

- Served on a Board of Directors;

- Was elected to leadership of scholarly associations;

- Advised or supervised undergraduate students;

- Advised or supervised graduate students;

- Served on thesis or dissertation committees (not as advisor or supervisor);

- Given talks or interviews for the general public; for example, TV, newspapers, and magazines.

Out of the fourteen opportunities, respondents reported participating in an average of 6.9. However, the average number of opportunities available to men (7.1) is statistically significantly higher than the average available to women (6.6). As with resources, we recognize that this difference could be due to factors other than gender. We ran a multiple regression model, and we found that discipline, age, employment sector, geographic region, and HDI explain some of the difference. The regression model results indicate that men have, on average, 0.2 more opportunities than women. Again, this is a small difference that can compound over a career.

3.5 Multivariate Analysis: Gender Differences in Discrimination and Career Choices and Progress as a Parent

In the first section, we examined gender differences in sexual harassment, and we found that women are much more likely to experience sexual harassment than men, even after accounting for potential confounding factors. In this section, we look at gender differences in discrimination. We also examine the differences in men's and women's choices about work/life balance and the impact of becoming a parent. Specifically, we examine differences in men's and women's responses to the following questions:

- *Never experienced discrimination.* I have never experienced discrimination.
- *Career influenced relationship decisions.* Has your career influenced your decisions about children, marriage, or a similar long-term partnership?
- *Promotion slowed after children.* My career or rate of promotion slowed significantly when I became a parent.
- *No career change after children.* My work or career did not change significantly when I became a parent.

Men are almost five times more likely never to have experienced discrimination than women. This holds after accounting for potential confounding factors such as age, disci-

Table 5: Gender differences in employment experiences as a parent.

Item	Gender Differences
Never experienced discrimination	**Men 4.8 times more likely** to **never have experienced discrimination** than women.
Career influenced relationship decisions	**Women 1.6 times** more likely to say **Yes** than men.
Promotion slowed after children	**Women 3.3 times more likely** to report **slower** rate of promotion after children than men.
No career change after children	**Men 3.0 times more likely** to report **no change after children** than women.

These gender differences are statistically significant at the $\alpha = 0.002$ level after accounting for potential confounding factors (age, discipline, geographic region, and level of development).

pline, employment sector, geographic region, and HDI. Women are also more likely to say that their career had influenced their decisions about marriage and children.

Finally, the effect of children on men's and women's career are vastly different. Women are about three times more likely to report slower rates of promotion after becoming a parent than men. This is consistent with the result that men are about three times more likely to report no change in career progress after becoming a parent.

A Closer Look at Gender Differences in Career Choices and Progress as a Parent by Discipline

As in the previous sections, we ran multivariate models for each discipline. We examine some of those findings below. We find that there is a statistically significant difference between men's and women's responses to whether their career influenced their decisions about children, marriage, or a similar long-term partnership by discipline (see Figure 28, p. 72).

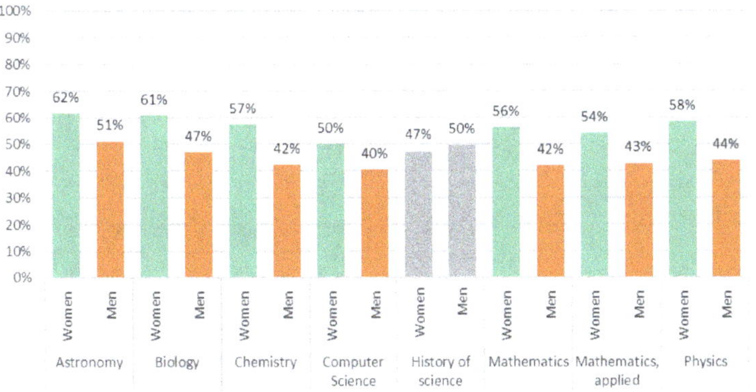

Each of these statistically significant relative differences (62% to 51%, or ~ 1.2 times, in Astronomy, for example) *understates* the relative likelihood between women and men in the multivariate model which accounts for confounding factors including age, employment sector, geographic region, and level of development.

Gray indicates the differences are not statistically significant by gender at the 0.002 level.

Figure 28: Percentages of respondents indicating their career influenced their decisions about children, marriage, or a similar long-term partnership by discipline.

We also find that there is a statistically significant difference in respondents' career or rate of promotion because they became a parent by discipline (see Figure 29, p. 73). A similar pattern emerges for respondents indicating their career had not changed significantly because they became a parent (Figure 30, p. 74).

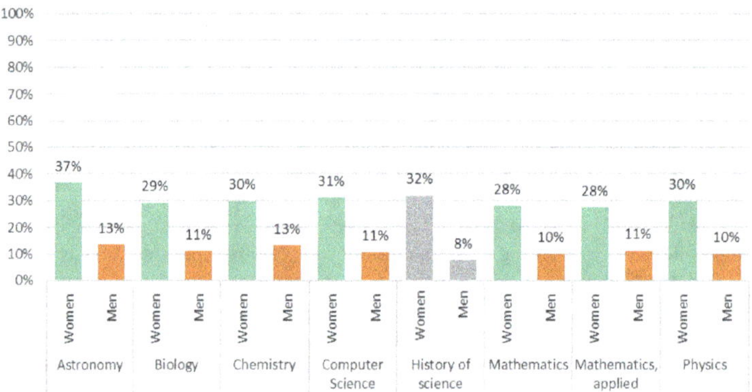

Each of these statistically significant relative differences (37% to 13%, or ~ 2.8 times, in Astronomy, for example) *understates* the relative likelihood between women and men in the multivariate model which accounts for confounding factors including age, employment sector, geographic region, and level of development.

Gray indicates the differences are not statistically significant by gender at the 0.002 level.

Figure 29: Percentages of respondents indicating their Career or rate of promotion slowed significantly because they became a parent by discipline.

A Closer Look at Gender Differences in Discrimination and Career Choices and Progress as a Parent by Geographic Region

Once again, we ran multivariate regression models for each geographic region. Men's careers were less likely to change after becoming a parent in every geographic region (see Figure 31, p. 75).

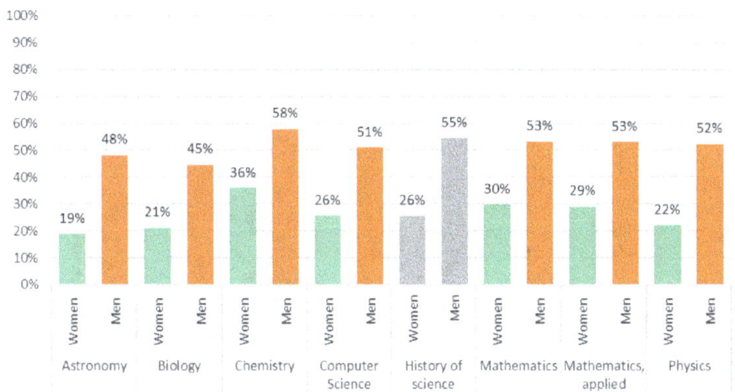

Each of these statistically significant relative differences (48% for men to 19% for women, or ~ 2.5 times, in Astronomy, for example) *understates* the relative likelihood between women and men in the multivariate model which accounts for confounding factors including age, employment sector, geographic region, and level of development.

Gray indicates the differences are not statistically significant by gender at the 0.002 level.

Figure 30: Percentages of respondents indicating their work or career did not changes significantly because they became a parent by discipline.

A Closer Look at Gender Differences in Discrimination and Career Choices and Progress as a Parent by Level of Development

Finally, we ran multivariate models for countries with higher and lower levels of economic development. We find men and women from countries with higher development levels respond differently to the questions about whether their career influenced decisions about their personal life; the same is not found in countries with lower levels of development (see Figure 32, p. 76). There is a statistically significant difference in the proportion of men and women indicating their work or career did not change significantly after becoming a parent (see Figure 33, p. 77).

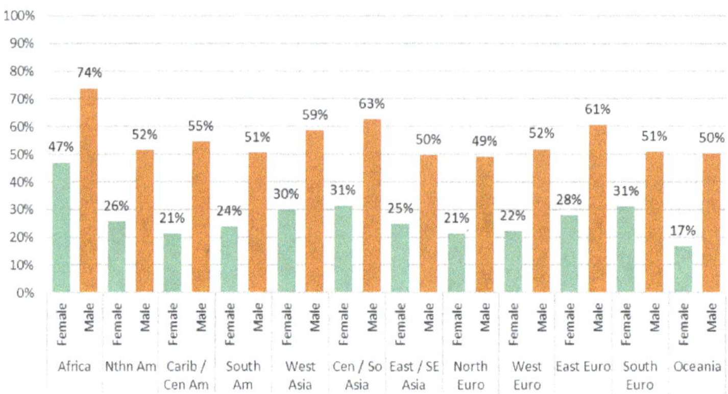

Each of these statistically significant relative differences (74% for men to 47% for women, or ~ 1.6 times, in Africa, for example) understates the relative likelihood between women and men in the multivariate model which accounts for confounding factors including age, employment sector, discipline, and level of development.

Figure 31: Percentages of respondents indicating their work or career did not change significantly after becoming a parent by geographic region.

3.6 Multivariate Analyses: Potential Areas to Examine

While our previous sections have focused on gender differences, we also used multivariate models to examine differences by discipline and by employment sector for potential lessons to be learned. We do not discuss all the differences we found below. Instead, we focus on areas where there are disciplines or employment sectors with more positive experiences than others. In those cases, there may be lessons to be learned. The analyses compare the differences for all respondents by discipline and by employment sector.

Selected Comparisons by Discipline

We tested for differences among responses by discipline after accounting for potential confounding factors including age, gender, employment sector, geographic region, and HDI. Selected results are highlighted in Table 6 (p. 78).

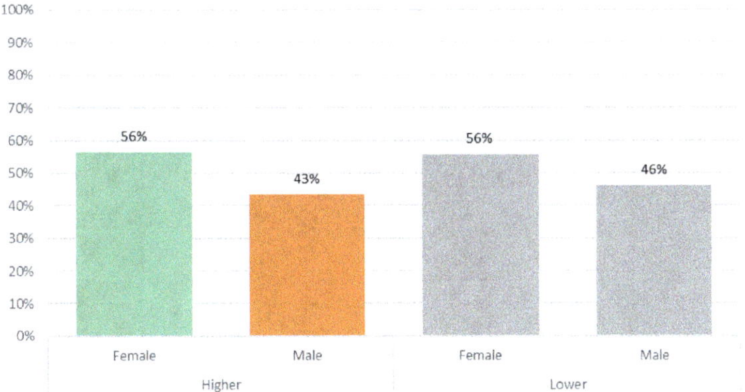

The statistically significant relative difference (56% for men to 43% for women, or ~ 1.3 times, in countries with higher levels of development, for example) understates the relative likelihood between women and men in the multivariate model which accounts for confounding factors including age, employment sector, discipline, and geographic region.

Gray indicates the differences are not statistically significant by gender at the 0.002 level.

Figure 32: Percentages of respondents indicating their career influenced their decisions about children, marriage, or a similar long-term partnership.

There may be lessons to be learned about advisor support from the responses about math programs, and there may be lessons to be learned about collegial relationships from employees who studied math and physics. Finally, respondents from math and chemistry were less likely to see a change in their careers after becoming a parent.

Selected Comparisons by Employment Sector

There may be lessons to learn from different employment sectors. The different employment sectors in which respondents reported working are:

- Academics
- Government or government entity
- Industry / private sector

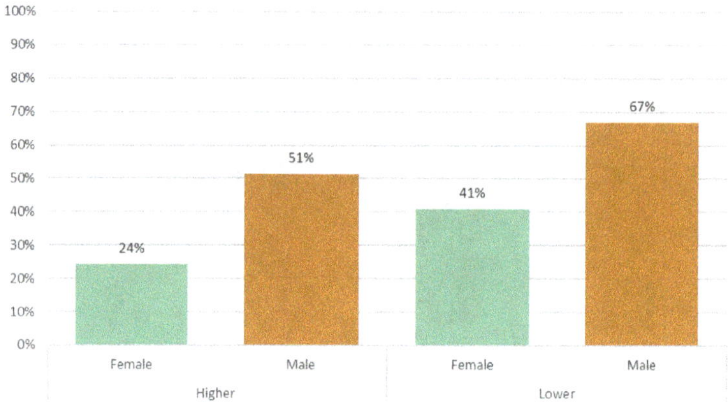

Figure 33: Percentages of respondents indicating their work or career did not change significantly after becoming a parent by level of development.

Both of the statistically significant relative differences (24% for women to 51% for men, or ~ 2 times, in countries with higher levels of development, for example) understate the relative likelihood between women and men in the multivariate model which accounts for confounding factors including age, employment sector, discipline, and geographic region.

- Non-governmental or non-profit organization

- Primary / secondary school

- Self-employed

- Other

We also examined differences across employment sectors. We found that respondents working in industry, non-governmental organizations and non-profits, primary / secondary schools, and respondents who were self-employed were more likely to report having respectful co-workers; those in government were less likely to do so. Respondents working in primary / secondary schools were more likely to say they had never experienced discrimination. These and other selected comparisons are highlighted in Table 7 (p. 79).

4 Discussion

These analyses provide compelling evidence that women and men do not have the same experiences in science, and that women's experiences are less positive than men's. There are gender differences in every area we examined:

- Women are more likely to report sexual harassment than men.

- Women are less likely than men to say that everyone is treated fairly in the educational system and in employment.

- Women report less positive relationships with their doctoral advisors, lower doctoral program quality, and more interruptions in doctoral studies than men.

- Women are less likely to report respectful treatment by co-workers than men. They are more likely than men to report slow career progression and discrimination.

Table 6: Disciplinary differences.

Item	Gender Differences
Doctoral advisor support[†]	Respondents from **Math** programs were **more likely** to rate advisor support **higher** than respondents from other disciplines.
Respectful co-workers[†]	Respondents whose discipline was **Physics** were **more likely** to **agree** they had respectful co-workers than respondents from other disciplines.
Never experienced discrimination[†]	Respondents from **Math** and **Physics** were **more likely** to indicate they had **never experienced discrimination** than respondents from other disciplines.
Promotion slowed after children[†]	Respondents from **Math** were **less likely** to indicate their **promotion slowed** after becoming a parent than respondents from other disciplines.
No career change after children[†]	Respondents from **Chemistry and Math** were **more likely** to indicate their work or career **did not change** when they became a parent than respondents form other disciplines.

These gender differences are statistically significant at the $\alpha = 0.002$ level after accounting for potential confounding factors (age, discipline, geographic region, and level of development).

[†] The dependent variable is ordinal, so we are unable to report a single odds ratio.

                                              The global survey of scientists

- Women have less access to career-advancing resources and opportunities than men.

- While women report better support from their families, the effect of children on women's careers is notable and not positive.

- Women are more likely than men to say that they relied on their own determination for their success in science.

Table 7: Employment sector differences.

Item	Gender Differences
Employer fair treatment[†]	Respondents working in **Government** were **less likely** to **agree**. Those working in **Industry, non-governmental or non-profit organizations, Primary / secondary schools** and those who were **self-employed** were **more likely** to **agree**. Respondents working in Academics and the "Other" sector were in between the two.
Respectful co-workers[†]	Respondents working in **Government** were **less likely** to **agree**. Those working in **Industry, non-governmental or non-profit organizations, Primary / secondary schools** and those who were **self-employed** were **more likely** to **agree**. Respondents working in Academics and the "Other" sector were in between the two.
Never experienced discrimination[†]	Respondents working in **Primary / secondary schools** were **more likely** to **agree** than respondents working in all other sectors.
Career influenced relationship decisions[†]	Respondents working in **Industry and Primary / secondary schools** were **more likely** to **agree** than respondents working in all other sectors.
Promotion slowed after children[†]	Respondents working in **Primary / secondary schools** were **less likely** to say their rate or promotion **slowed after children** than respondents working in all other sectors.
No career change after children[†]	Respondents working in **Government** and **Industry** were **more likely** to say their **career had not changed after children** than respondents working in all other sectors.

These gender differences are statistically significant at the $\alpha = 0.002$ level after accounting for potential confounding factors (age, discipline, geographic region, and level of development).

[†] The dependent variable is ordinal, so we are unable to report a single odds ratio.

There are other lessons to be learned. In examining doctoral programs, respondents studying in mathematics had a better perception of their advisor relationship than respondents in all other disciplines. Respondents studying computer science, mathematics, and physics were more likely to perceive they had been treated fairly in their graduate programs. Researchers can examine these programs for insight into why respondents felt this way.

In examining employment sectors, respondents working in industry, NGOs, primary/secondary schools, and who were self-employed were more likely to report having respectful co-workers than respondents working in academia. Respondents working in the government sector were least likely to report having respectful co-workers. Respondents working in industry and NGOs were more likely to report being treated fairly by their employers; this was also true for self-employed respondents. Respondents working in the government sector were less likely to report being treated fairly by their employer. Together these responses suggest that industry might have lessons to offer to other sectors on treatment of employees by co-workers and by managers.

5 Acknowledgements

The authors wish to thank Laura Merner and John Tyler for their invaluable contributions to the Global Survey of Scientists. We also wish to thank Marie-Françoise Roy and Mei-Hung Chiu for their leadership of this project. Finally, we thank all participants at the regional workshops who helped create the questionnaire.

References

[1] F. M. Dekking, C. Kraaikamp, H. P. Lopuhaä, and L. E. Meester. *A Modern Introduction to Probability and Statistics. Understanding Why and How.* London, UK: Springer, 2005. ISBN: 978-1-85233-896-1; 978-1-84996-952-9. DOI: 10.1007/1-84628-168-7.

[2] D. W. Jr. Hosmer, S. Lemeshow, and R. X. Sturdivant. *Applied Logistic Regression.* 3rd ed. New York, NY, USA: John Wiley & Sons, Inc., 2013. ISBN: 978-0-470-58247-3. DOI: 10.1002/9781118548387.

[3] R. Ivie and C. L. Tesfaye. "Women in physics: A tale of limits." In: *Physics Today* 65.2 (Feb. 2012), pp. 47–50. DOI: 10.1063/PT.3.1439. URL: https://www.aip.org/statistics/reports/global-survey-physicists.

[4] R. Ivie and S. White. "Is There a Land of Equality for Physicists? Results from the Global Survey of Physicists." In: *La Physique au Canada* 71.2 (2015), pp. 69–73.

[5] R. G. Jr. Miller. *Simultaneous Statistical Inference*. 2nd ed. New York, NY, USA: Springer, 1981. ISBN: 978-1-4613-8124-2. DOI: 10.1007/978-1-4613-8122-8.

[6] UNESCO. *Measuring gender equality in science and engineering: the SAGA survey of drivers and barriers to careers in science and engineering, SAGA Working Paper 4*. Paris, 2018. ISBN: 978-92-3-100300-4. URL: https://unesdoc.unesco.org/ark:/48223/pf0000266146.locale=en.

Measuring and Analyzing the Gender Gap in Science through the Joint Data-backed Study on Publication Patterns

Helena Mihaljević

Lucía Santamaría

Measuring and analyzing the gender gap in science through the joint data-backed study on publication patterns

Helena Mihaljevic [1], Lucía Santamaría[2]

1 – Hochschule für Technik und Wirtschaft (HTW) Berlin, University of Applied Science, Berlin, Germany
2 – Independent researcher, Berlin, Germany

Introduction

One of the three conceptual blocks of the Gender Gap in Science Project as defined in the funded proposal was the understanding of publication patterns in diverse academic fields and across world countries and regions, fundamentally with relation to the researchers' gender. This kind of analysis makes it possible to identify common and discipline-specific issues that might require interventions in view of the measured gender gap in STEM.

Successful academic careers are strongly tied to a prolific scholarly record; scientific publications are not only the major outlet for scholarly communication, they are regarded as a proxy for a researcher's scientific credo and play a key role in achieving and maintaining a successful career in academia. Decisions on tenure and other academic promotions are mostly based on evaluations of the candidate's research portfolio that pay special attention to research publications like journal articles, in addition to grants, conference presentations, and how visible or well-recognized a scholar is. Thus, the understanding of publication

---

Parts of this chapter will be proposed for publication as a peer-reviewed article, with an extended list of references.

practices in various STEM disciplines, obtained through measurable data on research output, is of great interest to academic institutions, science policy makers, and researchers alike.

1 Outline

In this report we first present an overview of our analysis methodology in Section 2: we present our data sources, discuss the schema used to count authors and authorships, describe how we extract author profiles and how we define academic cohorts, and discuss the processes employed to enrich our records with gender and geographical information. We then introduce in Section 3 the data visualization platform that we have built and that allows us to query data interactively. In Sections 4, 5, and 6 we break down analyses per discipline: for each of the fields of mathematics, astronomy and astrophysics, and theoretical physics we present a general overview of the situation of female researchers, putting, where possible, special emphasis on the influence of geographical factors and looking at its chronological evolution. In Section 7 we study the proportions of women in top journals per discipline, comparing insights from the global survey of scientists with those from actual bibliographic analyses. Finally, we summarize our results and compile our findings and recommendations for the project in Section 8.

2 Data and methods

2.1 Data sources

A key objective of the joint study on publication patterns was to create a sustainable and dynamic methodology to provide a continuous data processing flow, and hence allow for easy updates and longitudinal data analyses. To realize this objective and to be able to extract discipline-specific conclusions from bibliographic data, it is crucial to have access to high-quality, curated, comprehensive bibliographic collections on the fields of interest.

Our analysis of publication patterns is based on data from three bibliographic repositories managed by scientific organizations with a public interest. Their data are, at least partially, openly accessible.

- The SAO/NASA Astrophysics Data System[1] is a digital library for research in astronomy and astrophysics, operated by the Smithsonian Astrophysical Observatory (SAO) under a NASA grant. The analyses reflect the state of ADS at the end of March 2018.

- Zentralblatt MATH (zbMATH)[2] is the most comprehensive abstracting and reviewing service in pure and applied mathematics. zbMATH is produced by FIZ Karlsruhe, a member of the Leibniz Association, and as such a non-profit company. As was recently announced, zbMATH will be freely accessible from 2021.[3] Our analyses based on zbMATH capture the state of their database at the end of July 2019.

- The arXiv[4] provides open-access to e-prints in various fields, notably physics and mathematics but also in other disciplines such as computer science or quantitative biology. The arXiv is funded by Cornell University, the Simons Foundation and by member institutions. The analyses are based on data gathered from the arXiv at the end of July 2019.

We have further cross-referenced data from ADS and the arXiv with CrossRef[5] to enrich the information on serials and authors' first names. In the case of the arXiv this was especially useful because its e-prints do not include standardized information on the posterior appearance of articles in peer-reviewed journals.

For the field of chemistry, metadata on publications is provided through the Chemical Abstracts Service (CAS)[6], a subdivision of the American Chemical Society based in the USA. After the last Gender Gap in Science Project coordination meeting in Berlin, partners from IUPAC contacted CAS staff with the idea of integrating the data indexed by CAS into our analyses. Despite intensive efforts on both sides, it was not possible to reach a mutually feasible agreement for data exchange within the remaining project time. Since

---

[1] `https://ui.adsabs.harvard.edu`
[2] `https://zbmath.org`
[3] `https://www.fiz-karlsruhe.de/en/nachricht/`
   `zbmath-open-informationen-fuer-die-mathematik-werden-frei-zugaenglich`
[4] `https://arxiv.org`
[5] `https://www.crossref.org`
[6] `https://www.cas.org`

knowledge about the status of women chemists and their representation in chemistry publications remains scarce and incomplete ([3]), we have used the data from Crossref to investigate at least the proportion of women in 6 prestigious chemistry journals.

Arguably, many other bibliographic repositories and academic databases exist that could have potentially been used for the study on publication patterns. Our decision to restrict our analyses to the three mentioned above is rooted in several factors. Firstly, the issue of data accessibility is not trivial: many bibliographic services operate under a subscription model that does not allow free queries and downloads. Moreover, their licenses might forbid the creation of derived data artifacts like the ones constructed in our investigations. Secondly, data completeness and cleanliness is key to achieve trustworthy results. Many academic databases are either not complete, therefore can't be used to illustrate the state of a scientific field, or their data are not of enough quality (i.e. missing metadata, author information, etc.) to warrant an appropriate analysis. The data sources selected by us are certainly not perfect either. For example, zbMATH and arXiv.org only partially provide authors' affiliations. Furthermore, the arXiv does not offer author profiles and, as a preprint repository, it only partially reflects the state of published literature in physics. Collaborations of applied mathematicians outside of mathematics are certainly not completely represented in zbMATH. Nevertheless, all three are comprehensive and (very) well maintained sources for scientific publications in the mentioned disciplines. Finally there is the question of availability of resources within such a research project: in that respect we regard the computer science database DBLP[7] as a highly suitable data source for corresponding studies of publication practices in computer science but due to lack of time we were not able to include it in our analyses.

That said, our choice of data sources offers a unique and complete glimpse into the fields of mathematics, astronomy and astrophysics, and theoretical physics. It provides a solid starting point for the understanding of the gender dynamics and developments in STEM publishing over the past 40 years.

---

[7]`https://dblp.uni-trier.de`

2.2 Authors and authorships

Academic publications are authored by one or various individuals (=authors); formally speaking, we consider each one-to-many pair of publication and author as one instance of *authorship*. For example, an article authored by three individuals yields three different authorships that we try to assign to three different authors. (The creation of such author profiles is explained in the following section.)

Authorships might be counted in various ways: typically they are weighted equally, regardless of the total number of authors in the paper and with no distinction on the order of appearance. This leads to a counting scheme that does not discriminate between authorships of a single-author article and those of a large collaboration. Alternatively, one can incorporate the importance of publishing solo by computing so-called *fractional authorships*, where each authorship is assigned a weight of $1/n$, with n being the total number of authors. (In the above example of three individuals writing together one article, each of the authorships would be weighted by $1/3$.) Furthermore, analyses can be made that consider only one specific position in the list of authors as relevant, and often it is the first or the last slot that has a particularly important meaning.

The sensible choice of counting schema for authorships is highly field-specific and depends on the peculiarities of each discipline. In mathematics there are very few large collaborations, most articles being written by a handful of authors. In that situation, statistics on publication patterns remain roughly unchanged when using equal or fractional authorship counts. This is not the case in other fields like astronomy or high-energy physics though, where sizeable collaborations abound; hence in those cases it makes more sense to compare with fractional authorships.

To find out further insights on publications practices in different disciplines, we resort to the global survey of scientists described in Chapter , specifically the following question: *"In your field, which criteria are usually used to determine who will be the first, middle, or last author?"*. Almost half of the 27,732 respondents answered with "relative contribution", followed by "alphabetical ordering". Details are displayed in Figure 1 (p. 90).

Publication customs regarding the assignment of author order vary per discipline: in mathematics the dominant criterion is alphabetical, but this is a fairly uncommon practice everywhere else, even being practically unheard of in biology and chemistry. In those areas, it is not uncommon that the last position in the author list is automatically granted to

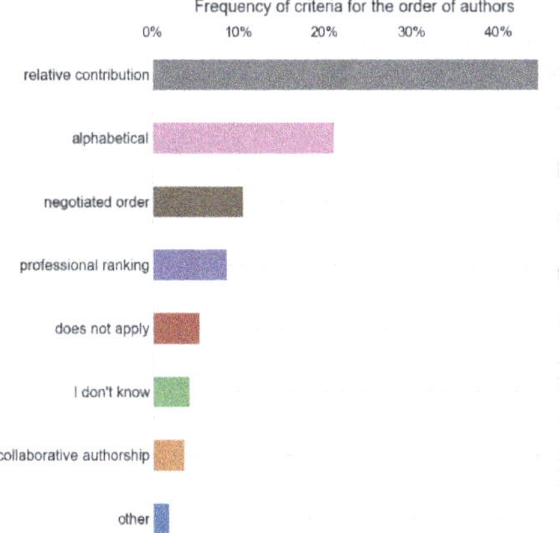

Figure 1: Distribution of answers to the question *"In your field, which criteria are usually used to determine who will be the first, middle, or last author?"* from the global survey of scientists.

the PI or director of the laboratory where experiments were conducted. In other fields, particularly in astronomy, the relative contribution of each author to the work is the most common reason to list authors in a particular order. See Figure 2 (p. 91) for actual numbers obtained from the global survey's respondents. In fact, astronomy has its particular unspoken publication policies, whereby whoever did most of the work becomes first author, usually followed by a small number of major contributors. Equal (smaller) contributors are listed next in alphabetical order. Generally speaking, when subsequent authors are not alphabetical, the order reflects the importance of their contributions. Both first and leading (second or third) authors play important roles.

Publication practices regarding author lists vary by field and it is thus necessary to choose the right authorship counting schema when dealing with data from different repositories.

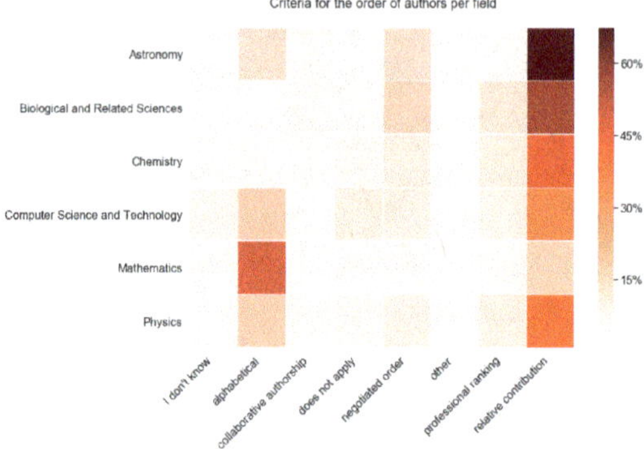

Figure 2: Heatmap displaying the distribution of answers to the question *"In your field, which criteria are usually used to determine who will be the first, middle, or last author?"* from the global survey of scientists, broken down by academic discipline.

2.3 Author profiles

Bibliographic databases contain large compilations of research articles' metadata as released by the publisher. This includes fields such as title, authors' names and affiliations, publication venue and date, and others. Only infrequently are records also disambiguated to assess the identity of their individual authors. The creation of author profiles from bibliographic records, i.e. the construction of clusters to agglutinate all publications of a given researcher, is essential to perform analyses on scholarly data to the level of individuals. Without this intricate process, also known as "author name disambiguation", research articles can not be linked to each other on the basis of common authors; thus aggregations per scientists' gender that enable answering questions on gender issues are unfeasible.

Author name disambiguation is a rather ambiguous and challenging task. Usually, metadata associated to the authors' names and affiliation is incomplete (e.g. abbreviated first names) or vague (e.g. abridged institutional information). As a consequence, authorship attribution suffers from various well-known issues such as confusion of authors with frequent names, missing name parts, variability through transliteration, or name changes throughout a researcher's life. The inclusion of further data facets, such as affiliations, coauthor graphs, subject field, or keywords makes it possible to infer authorships more accurately. Author disambiguation can be done on the basis of manual work, rule-based approaches, collaborative input (i.e. community-based) or Machine Learning (ML) techniques. In the latter case, a fair amount of labeled records is needed to train a model that can learn to automatically disambiguate unseen data.

For the purpose of our study on publication patterns we proceeded as follows: mathematics database zbMATH does provide author profiles, whereas ADS and the arXiv lack this feature. zbMATH author profiles are constructed via rule-based, manual, and collaborative methods, and could be directly employed for our analysis. For disambiguation of the ADS records we have instead trained an ML model on manually disambiguated data and we combined it with heuristics to fine-tune the resulting author profiles. In the case of the arXiv we have implemented a known initial-based approach by [17], which yields sufficiently accurate results given our data. This approach might be replaced by our trained ML model in the future, after suitable evaluations have been performed.

2.4 Academic cohorts

A cohort is a group of individuals that share a common characteristic over a defined period of time. Comparing the development of cohorts allows for longitudinal studies that unveil patterns over large periods of time. We were most interested in following the development of women and men researchers over the years, making use of our data sources that partially date back to the 1970s. Thus, in our study, we assigned authors to a given cohort according to the year of first recorded publication, which acts as an approximation for the beginning of their scientific career. In this way we could follow the publication records of all authors in every cohort and select those individuals that continue publishing a set number of years after their first paper. Depending on the discipline it might for instance be reasonable to roughly assume researchers to be at the postdoctoral stage 5 years after their first publication and to have secured a permanent position at professorial level another 5 years later.

2.5 Gender inference

Bibliographic metadata do not include the authors' gender, thus this information needs to be inferred. Usually, an author's name is the only piece of information capable of providing an indication of their gender. For the present data we have combined responses from different gender assignment services, maximizing the recall (i.e. the number of names that can be assigned a gender), while keeping the error rate under a certain threshold. Our algorithm is based on a published benchmark [20] where we compared five dedicated web services and software packages. Roughly speaking, in a first stage we use the assignments from Gender API[8] that features a high probability score. For names leading to probability values between 75 and 90 in Gender API, we combined responses with those from genderize.io[9]. All remaining unidentified first names were processed with Python package gender guesser[10], which had shown high precision but low recall. For authors without a first name but whose names appear in the Wikipedia list of Soviet surnames[11], we applied surname ending rules to infer the gender.

Numerous challenges arise in connection with automated gender inference (AGR). To name a few, the association of a name with gender is not unique and also depends on the cultural and regional context, hence relying on the first name only can be highly error-prone and lead to a bias towards certain countries. Transliteration from other alphabets into the Latin one is known to lead to significant losses of information, thereby excluding entire populations from a reliable classification. Furthermore, all AGR approaches that build on names or other physiological features, such as facial images or voice, assume a binary definition of gender that reinforces a non-inclusive gender concept. Despite these (and other) critiques, we have performed a name-based gender inference since academia is notoriously not gender-agnostic and because relevant gender differences can be observed and need to be explained. We have discussed various issues related to AGR in [15] and would welcome ideas towards more inclusive concepts, preferably based on self-identification. Those would allow fairer, sustainable and statistically significant analyses of bibliographic corpora in terms of gender.

As a result of the gender assignment procedure, all author names are tagged with a 'female', 'male', or 'unknown' qualifier. The percentage of non-labeled records is generally large (see 4.1, 5.1, and 6.1) and primarily affects names from certain regions; for instance, authors of Chinese ancestry are more often assigned unknown labels due to loss of gen-

---

[8]`https://gender-api.com`
[9]`https://genderize.io`
[10]`https://github.com/lead-ratings/gender-guesser`
[11]`https://en.wikipedia.org/wiki/List_of_surnames_in_Russia`

der marking during transliteration. In our analyses in relation to gender we removed all authorships from authors with unknown gender, which introduces a selection bias. An agnostic estimation of the incurred error would assume that the percentage of men and women in the unknown group mimics the ratio between the groups identified as male and female. Yet, we know from our previous studies [16] that the proportion of women in the group of authors labeled unknown is smaller than the share of identified females. This means that non-labeled names are more likely to be men than women. Thus we conclude that our estimated percentage of women among all authorships when removing unknown authors is always an upper bound with respect to the entire data set of authors. When possible, we have added error regions to our plots to reflect this fact.

2.6 Extraction of geo-information

A major focus of the Gender Gap in Science Project is the consideration of worldwide data to produce insights and recommendations for all geographical world areas. Results of the project should highlight contrasts and common ground across regions and cultures, less developed and highly developed countries, thus promoting an inclusive view of STEM researchers. To realize this goal, the database of publications needs to be enriched with geo-information, which is most readily available from the authors' affiliations.

Our data sources have different levels of coverage regarding institutional affiliations: in ADS about 80% of all authorships have an affiliation[12], whereas in the arXiv this information is rarely available[13]. In zbMATH, the metadata on publications from the past decade are the main source of affiliations, but they are available at the level of articles, not of authorships. This means that a one-to-one correlation between each author of an article and an affiliation is missing, thus the information can be used only partially.

We extracted geo-information via a multi-level algorithmic procedure, based on the following steps: (1) extraction of locations using the Stanford Named Entity Recognizer (NER)[14], (2) queries to the database GeoNames[15] and (3) parsing of the affiliation strings

---

[12]https://gender-gap-in-science.org/2018/03/17/
   mining-50-years-of-astronomy-and-astrophysics-publications-data/
[13]https://gender-gap-in-science.org/2017/07/19/
   a-fresh-first-look-at-the-arxiv-data/
[14]https://nlp.stanford.edu/software/CRF-NER.html
[15]http://www.geonames.org/

with CERMINE[16], an ML based software for extracting meta-information from academic publications. By aggregating countries according to the main world regions, the inferred geo-information enabled us to restrict our analyses to different geographical areas as foreseen in the project's goals.

The analyses presented in this report were carried out at country level. In subsequent publications and projects, we plan to extend this to a more granular level.

3 Website with interactive visualizations

A key objective of the Gender Gap in Science Project is the creation of a sustainable and dynamic methodology to provide a continuous data processing flow and enable easy updates and longitudinal data analyses. Academic studies are generally static and on occasion leave the door open to follow-up questions that are left unaddressed in the conclusions. On the contrary, our project intends to be sustainable and aims at making data available to interested audiences. As argued in [15], scientometrics has the potential to influence researchers' careers and lives. Since bibliographic data are often closed and stored in pay-walled corpora, considerable efforts should be made into finding compromises with the rightholders of databases that allow for transparent evaluations. Opening up the data sources and granting access to more granular statistics than what is traditionally contained in a regular publication greatly encourages custom analyses that go above and beyond the original research questions. This in turn is a fantastic incentive to explore further research topics and benefit the scientometrics community. Essentially, such a transparent approach contributes to the much needed democratization of data and its removal from data silos.

A major effort of our work has thus been to build and maintain an open platform that allows ad-hoc analyses of bibliographic data with relation to gender. The resulting webpage can be accessed via its public URL `http://gender-publication-gap.f4.htw-berlin.de/`. The site provides structured access to publication data from STEM disciplines in relation to the gender of the publishing authors. Building on previous work [16], our visualizations address several crucial aspects for understanding the impact of publication patterns on the gender gap:

---

[16]`https://github.com/CeON/CERMINE`

- Research activity over time. Based on aggregated data by cohorts, it is possible to visualize the share of authors and authorships in publications from zbMATH, ADS and the arXiv, as well as the drop-out rate and the gender publication gap.

- Share of women and men in different journals. All serials stored in the three analyzed databases can be individually queried to reveal the share of authors per gender and publication year. Additionally, several journals can be selected and compared, which enables analysis of specific research fields by means of their most representative journals.

- Distribution across sub-fields. Publications within a scientific discipline are typically subclassified into subjects according to specific schemas. Bibliographic records are classified by their topical schema, which makes it possible to study gender dynamics in different subfields.

- Joint impact of gender and geographical location. Country-level information extracted from authors' affiliations can be accessed, making it possible to investigate gender differences by country.

The aim of the interactive platform is to encourage analyses that contribute to a better understanding of the interplay between a scientist's gender and their scholarly output. By providing dynamic visualizations we wish to enable researchers, scientific organizations, policy makers, as well as the interested general public to explore the data, formulate new hypotheses, and derive evidence for informed decisions. The Gender Publication Gap website will be available even after completion of the Gender Gap in Science Project.

4 Mathematics

We present our analysis of the field of mathematics based on the data from zbMATH from 1970 to July 2019. We put special emphasis into characterizing the discipline and providing geo-specific information. We then expose our findings in relation to gender.

4.1 Methodology

Definition of core mathematics

zbMATH is a comprehensive database that indexes publications from all areas of pure mathematics as well as its applications, in particular to natural sciences, computer science, economics and engineering. It also covers history and philosophy of mathematics as well as university education. The broad coverage of zbMATH results in the fact that also publications of scientists working primarily in another discipline are indexed, and thus possibly only a fraction of their publications is indexed in zbMATH. For a focused analysis on mathematics practitioners and their academic career paths, it is sensible to first reduce the data set to so-called core mathematics. Below we define the heuristics that we have employed to implement said filter.

Entries in zbMATH are classified according to the Mathematics Subject Classification Scheme (MSC 2010), a tree-like, three-level alphanumerical scheme to label publications according to their subject matter. The MSC exists since 1970; it is revised every 10 years, with MSC 2010 being the current version[17], which will be updated in 2020. Articles classified with first-level MSC codes between 03 and 65 belong to mathematics subfields such as Logic, Discrete Mathematics, Algebra, Analysis, Geometry, Topology, Probability Theory, Statistics, and Numerical Mathematics. Those with codes between 68 and 94 fall into mathematical applications related to Computer Science, Physics, or Economics. The areas 00 and 01 refer to general topics and history of mathematics; 97 is Mathematical Education.

For every journal in the database we computed the percentage of its articles in a core MSC class, this is, between 03 and 65. If that percentage was larger than 90%, then said serial was considered as a *core mathematics journal*. Additionally, all journals indexed in zbMATH cover-to-cover were also considered in this group, as confirmed by the expert opinion of their editorial board. Finally, all articles published before 1970 were also tagged as core mathematics, since that was the focus of the indexing service back then. As a result of this procedure, any article from a core mathematics journal was considered mathematics, and any person who had published a core mathematics article was considered a mathematician. For every mathematician, however, we considered their full publication record (including

---

[17]http://msc2010.org/Default.html

articles potentially not in core mathematics journals) in author-centered analyses, e.g. when looking at cohorts or collaboration networks. Our approach allows for a broad definition of mathematicians and mathematical publications without including authors in our analysis that appear in zbMATH but actually publish mostly in satellite areas.

Data overview

For the study of mathematics we resort to the full collection of publications authored by core mathematicians from 1970 until July 2019. This data set comprises 3,083,185 documents corresponding to 5,273,035 instances of authorship, yielding an average of 1.7 authors per article. Among these authorships, 3,592,745 were assigned to men, 471,823 to women, and 1,193,467 could not be assigned to any gender. Omitting the 'unknown' group, authorships of women accounted for about 12% of all authorships to which we could assign a gender. Due to the availability of author profiles in zbMATH, no name disambiguation procedure needed to be implemented to cluster all authorships into individual researcher profiles. We have applied our gender assignment algorithm as described in 2.5 to 471,277 author profiles and were able to assign a gender to 149,557 (68%) of all of them; among those, 64,887 (21%) authors were labeled as women and 256,833 (79%) as men.

Categorization of mathematical journals

Rather than resorting to external journal rankings to differentiate among perceived quality of mathematics serials, we adopted instead zbMATH's internal processing schema. Its purpose is the categorization of journals, reflecting the relevance of their contents for mathematics and particular subfields. Their schema, which consists of a handful of categories, is not public and is updated on a regular basis by zbMATH's editorial staff and a group of experts from a multitude of fields. In addition to the categorization of journals in groups, a total of 1271 serials have been or still are indexed cover-to-cover, i.e. all their articles are imported into the database, automatically conferring them a high-relevance status. Finally, a selected group of 175 "priority" serials are given preferential treatment due to their assumed novelty and special relevance. Based on this classification procedure, we have constructed two data sets, "Core Math" and "Core Math Priority"[18], to discriminate

---

[18] Editorial prioritization can certainly change over time, and a journal that was not considered particularly valuable 20 years ago may well have a different reputation today. However, experience shows that the

among journals: one containing all core mathematics serials and another restricted to the prioritized ones. The latter is deemed to contain only highly renowned publication venues of proven quality. To give an estimate of the proportions, the articles in "Core Math Priority" made up about 25% of the "Core Math" dataset in the last 10 years.

4.2 Results

General statistics

The field of mathematics has been growing significantly over the past decades, and this fact is reflected on the amount of research output. Approximately 15,000 mathematics articles, featuring about 25,000 authorships, used to appear per year during the decade of 1970. The number of yearly articles in core mathematics has quadrupled ever since, having practically doubled over the past 20 years and currently reaching over 60,000 items and 140,000 authorships per year, as shown in Figure 3. Yet, this phenomenal growth is hardly comparable to that in computer science, where technological progress and high demands on the job market have given the discipline an enormous push.

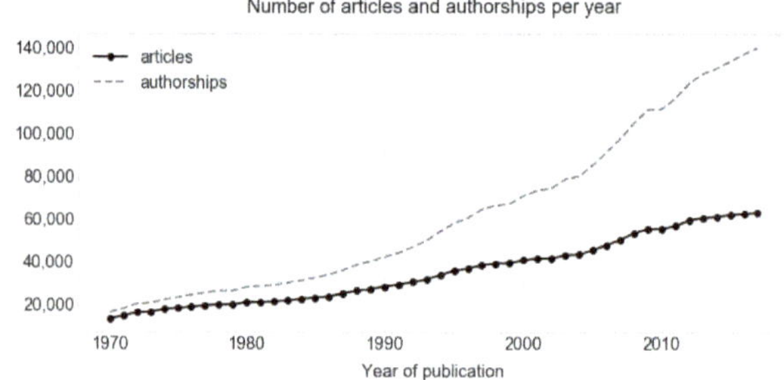

Figure 3: Number of published articles and corresponding authorships per year in mathematics as indexed by zbMATH.

Publication trends in mathematics indicate a rise in collaborative practices among researchers: while in the 1970s the majority of articles, more than three quarters, were

corresponding fluctuations are rather small in mathematics, so that we can assume a relatively high stability here.

single-authored, mathematics papers nowadays feature just over two authors on average. Single authorships now account for about one quarter of all publications, as do articles with three authors; the majority of publications are collaborations of two authors, while articles with four or more remain infrequent. Figure 4 (p. 100) clearly shows the steady decline of single-authored publications and the corresponding rise of coauthorships.

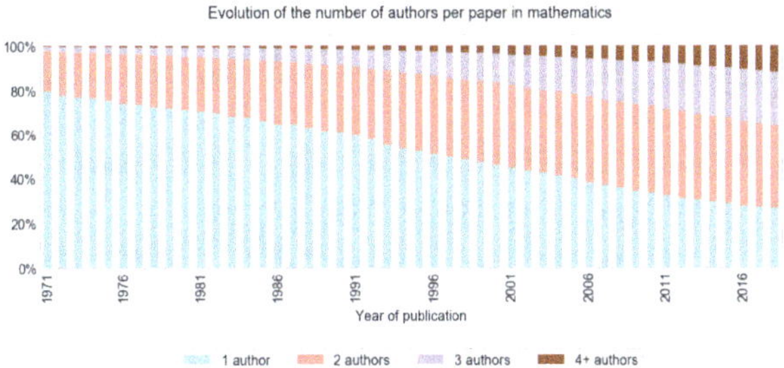

Figure 4: Evolution of the number of authors per paper in mathematics since 1970.

Geographical insights

A major point of interest for the Gender Gap in Science Project is the analysis of data with input from various geographical regions, as this kind of information shall shed light on the role played by different world areas in the shaping of the situation of women in STEM. Below we present several analyses based on geo-information that has been extracted from the affiliations of published articles.

Coverage of country information

The availability of geo-information matched to publications is dependent on the amount and quality of accessible affiliations in the database. The efforts of zbMATH to index them are relatively recent, having built up mostly over the past decade. Accordingly, the coverage is not as complete and granular as in other sources such as the ADS. The majority of affiliations in zbMATH are stored only on the level of articles, i.e. for multi-authored publications it is often not possible to assign one affiliation to each individual author.

More concretely, publishers become a source of possible selection bias, as the quality of delivered affiliations varies among them. In practice this means that certain publishers can spend more resources to ensure that their affiliations are processed such that zbMATH can properly harvest them. Consequently, zbMATH has better coverage of geo-information for journals from large companies than for those from smaller publishers that lack those capabilities.

To better assess the potential bias in the coverage of the authors' country of work we have analyze two data sets: Core Math contains all articles in core mathematics journals (see definition in 4.1), whereas Core Math Priority is a subset of the former restricted to articles in zbMATH's prioritized journals group. For both sets we studied articles from the years 2009-2018, when affiliation data in zbMATH is consistently available. Set Core Math comprises 617,271 articles from 1,230 distinct journals, while the smaller set contains 158,163 from only 175 serials.

Next, we report some facts about our coverage of geo-information in relation to publishers. For a clearer overview we have merged individual publishers into larger publishing groups, thus e.g. all Springer and Elsevier local entities have been combined, respectively. In Core Math Springer and Elsevier make up 45% of all articles; in Core Math Priority their share is even higher. Figure 5 shows the top 15 publishers in Core Math and the percentage of articles for which at least one country could be extracted. The coverage with country information is generally large; for Springer, Elsevier and AMS it is in fact above 80%. Three major publishers, however, do not contribute country information, namely SIAM, IEE and IMS.

Figure 6 (p. 102) displays the bias in coverage of country information. The light-colored bars represent the percentage of articles per publisher when considering the whole Core Math set, whereas the darker shade is restricted to articles with available geo-information. It is noticeable that larger publishing groups Springer and Elsevier are overrepresented in our sample; this result extends to the smaller Core Math Priority set.

Figure 7 focuses on said major publishers, Springer and Elsevier, plus two traditional, high-quality university and society publishing houses, the American Mathematical Society and Cambridge University Press. For each of them we show the 10 most common countries taken from their affiliations. A notable difference is the presence of authors working in China: these constitute the largest group in Elsevier publications (18%), while comprising

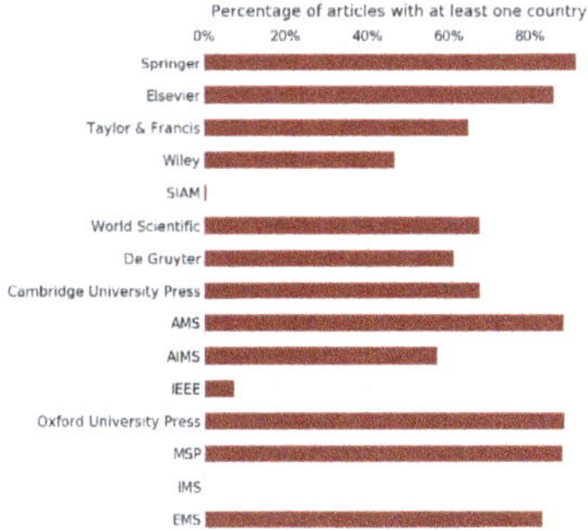

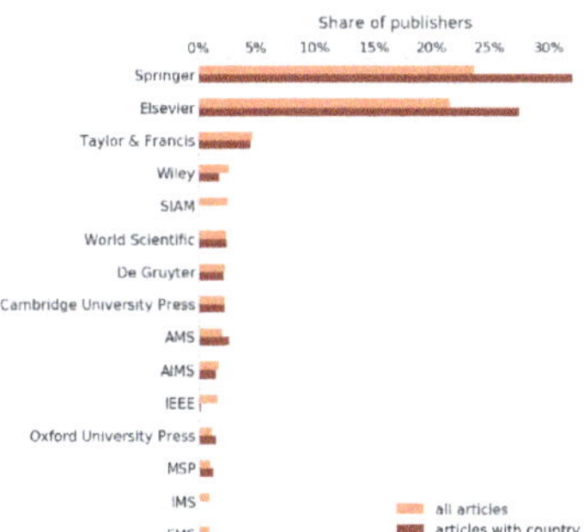

Figure 5: Percentage of articles with extracted country information from affiliations from the top 15 publishers in zbMATH's Core Math data set.

Figure 6: Bias in coverage of country information. Light bars indicate the share of total articles per publisher and dark ones restrict to those containing geo-information.

only about 6% in journals of the AMS. The USA is the second most frequent country in journals from large publishers, making up for 12-13%, whereas it is by far the most common country in articles published by the AMS (almost 30% of all their authors work in the USA). All four publishers have similar countries among their top 10.

Next we apply the same analysis to the Core Math Priority data set, which comprises highly renowned journals in mathematics. Results are displayed in Figure 8. Restricting to them, the USA appears as the most frequent country in all cases, while the proportion of authors in China decreases significantly with respect to the full Core Math data set.

Undoubtedly, the plots above indicate that there exists a bias in the coverage of countries per article due to the differences in metadata delivery of affiliations and corresponding parsing of them in zbMATH. It is nevertheless almost unfeasible to quantify exactly how large this bias is. For our further analyses regarding geo-information it is important to bear in mind that (1) one can not simply extrapolate the number of mathematicians per country from the distribution of the author countries in the existing publication data and that (2) our country analyses mirror quite exactly what the situation is in the majority of publications in mathematics, in particular regarding Springer and Elsevier but also in many

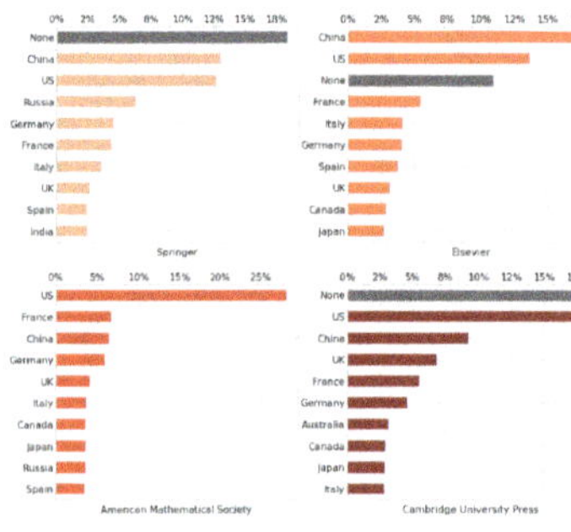

Figure 7: Distribution of countries in publications from four major publishers contained in the Core Math data set.

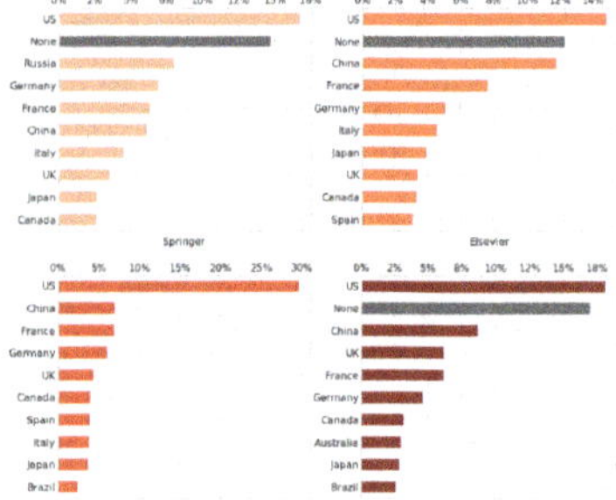

Figure 8: Distribution of countries in publications from four major publishers contained in the Core Math Priority data set.

smaller publishing houses. Yet, some publishers like SIAM or IEEE are underrepresented and for those we can not exactly say which part of the picture is missing.

Geographical distribution of publications in core mathematics

The above-mentioned caveats notwithstanding, it is still possible to gain significant understanding of current regional trends in mathematics by studying research output per world area. We therefore concentrate on publications from the past 10 years and the extracted countries from the corresponding available author affiliations. For 30% of the publications in zbMATH's Core Math data set no country could be ascertained (see 4.2); that figure drops to 27% for publications in the Core Math Priority data set. For the remaining 70% articles in Core Math and 73% in Core Math Priority for which the country can be determined, the choropleth maps in Figures 9 (p. 104) and 10 illustrate their geographical distribution.

Over the past decade, China and USA have completely led research in core mathematics, as 19% and 16% of publications with assigned country, respectively, originate from those two countries. Central- and South Europe, in addition to Russia, India, Japan, and Canada follow, yet with considerably smaller contributions in the range of 3-6% of the total. A handful of countries including Brazil, Australia, Iran, Turkey, and Poland supply 1-2% of all

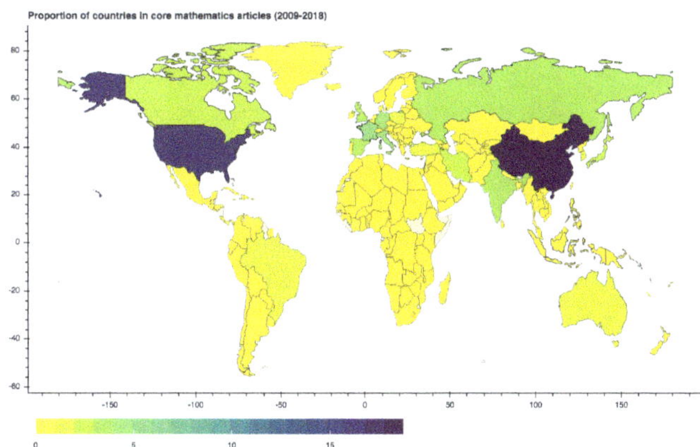

Figure 9: Proportion of countries of work from the authors of mathematical articles from zb-MATH's Core Math data set in 2009-2018

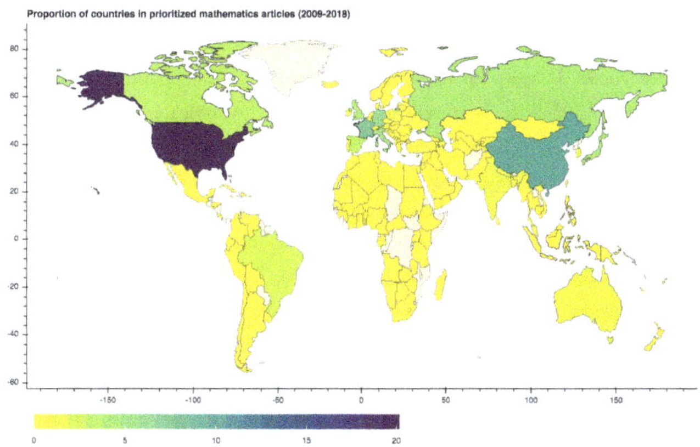

Figure 10: Proportion of countries of work from the authors of mathematical articles from zb-MATH's Core Math Priority data set in 2009-2018.

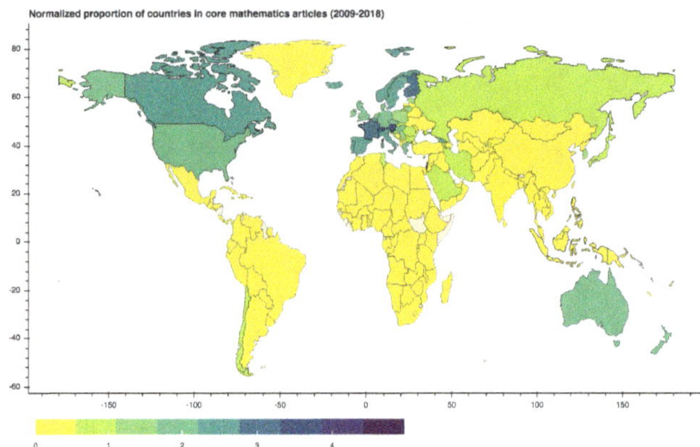

Figure 11: Proportion of countries of work from the authors of mathematical articles from zb-MATH's Core Math data set in 2009-2018, normalized by the average population size in the respective country in the same period of time.

geo-enriched articles. Below that threshold are the majority of countries, most notably the entirety of Africa, Western and Central Asia, and Central America, plus all South America excluding Brazil. When restricting to publications in the smaller and more exclusive Core Math Priority dataset as shown in Figure 10 we observe that the presence of China decreases, whereas the USA keeps its leading position.

Figures 9 and 10 clearly highlight the utter dominance of China and the USA in core mathematics in absolute numbers in the analyzed time period 2009-2018. Obviously, demographics play a significant role in these results, as it is natural to expect that their larger populations of mathematicians will contribute more articles overall. Thus we have normalized the figures by averaged country population size during 2009-2018 and this gives rise to the data displayed in Figure 11. As it turns out, there is a handful of countries with small populations that nevertheless contribute a substantial amount to core mathematics publications. In fact, the largest normalized proportion stems from Israel, closely followed by Slovenia, Luxembourg, and Austria, which hints at the existence of comparatively strong mathematical communities in those countries.

Strength of international collaborations in mathematics

A natural question is whether mathematicians from different countries are connected among them through common research lines and published research, and if so, which geographical areas have the strongest international ties. To illustrate this issue, we have looked at publications from zbMATH's Core Math subset written by two authors for which we were able to extract both researchers' countries of work from their affiliations (see caveats about bias of this approach in Section 4.2). From the obtained data set we have removed articles from authors working in the same country, leaving only the international collaborations.

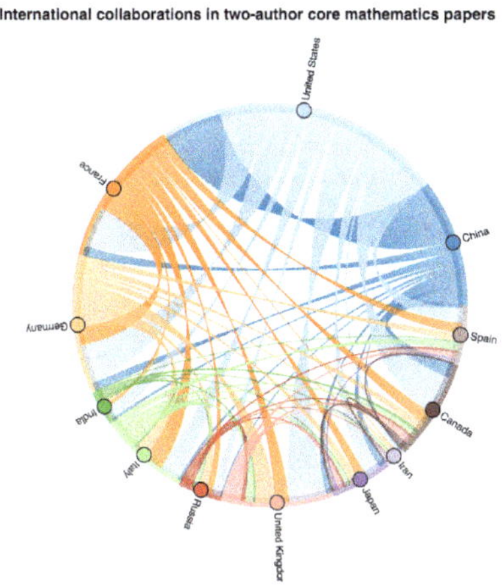

Figure 12: Depiction of the number of articles from zbMATH's Core Math dataset written by two authors from different countries represented as connecting arcs between said countries.

Figure 12 shows the number of international coauthorship relations between pairs of mathematicians from the 12 most frequent countries, displayed as connecting arcs. A rich pattern emerges, confirming that mathematicians from all countries regularly cooperate internationally (less frequent countries have been omitted from the plot to avoid clogging it). It is interesting to note that about half of the international publications from China are written with mathematicians from the USA, whereas the opposite is not true. Although the USA-China relation is strong, USA researchers also work frequently with scientists in France, Germany, the UK, and Canada, and comparatively less with India, Russia, and Iran. Overall, this plot hints at a large amount of international collaboration in the field of mathematics.

Gender analysis in mathematics

Active female mathematicians

In addition to the growing amount of research output mentioned in Section 4.2, the number of individual authors that publish in mathematics has increased considerably within the time frame of our analysis. Part of this trend is certainly due to the increment in mathematical applications (and correspondingly broader indexing in zbMATH); in addition, the changing publishing habits surely play an important role too, as it has become common practice to submit scientific papers already during the doctoral period and not afterwards as was the norm a few decades ago. This fact, combined with the increment of graduate programs in mathematics worldwide, helps explain the rising number of authors.

Regarding the gender of mathematics practitioners, it is remarkable to point out that the proportion of women among them has also increased steadily, growing from less than 10% for the 1970s cohorts to over 27% nowadays. Figure 13 indicates that over 14,000 new mathematicians have published their first scientific paper in 2018; this corresponds to an estimated number of almost 4,000 female mathematicians entering the field yearly.

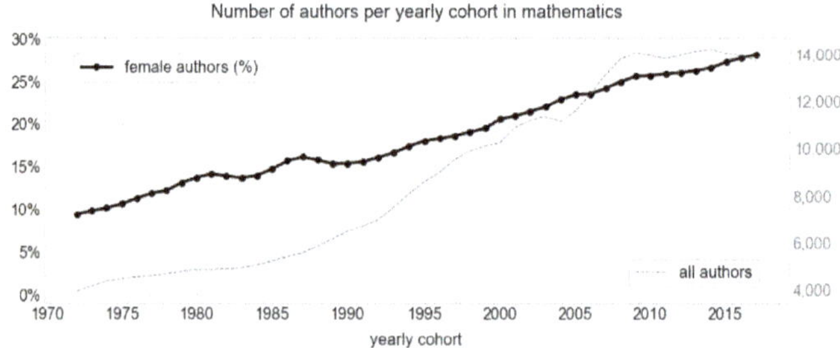

Figure 13: Number of active (publishing) mathematicians since 1970 and percentage of them that are women.

Career length of men and women in mathematics

Next we set to analyze whether there exist variations in the standard publishing career length of women and men in mathematics. We assume that a given author has been publishing for a set amount of X years, if we can find a corresponding publication in the zbMATH database X years after their first paper. For a given number of years X (e.g. 5 if we want to have a proxy for a post-doctoral stage), we compute the percentage of researchers that are still active for another Y years. This way we can estimate the amount of researchers per cohort that continues in academia after a certain amount of time. Figure 14 shows, for cohorts from 1970 until 2003, the share of men (left) and women (right) who are active for another 1 to 10 years after having published academic articles for 5 years. We have applied window smoothing to get a cleaner picture of the displayed data.

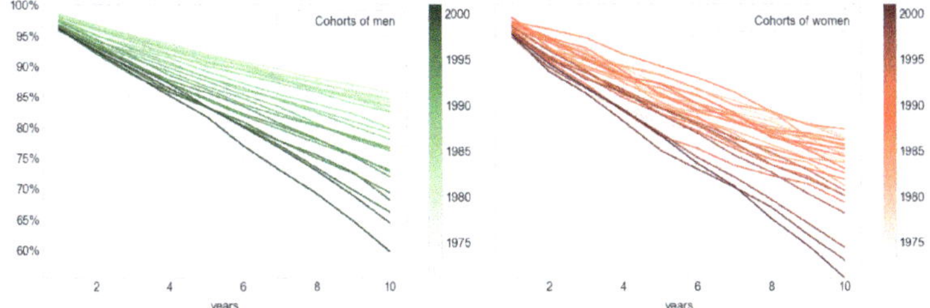

Figure 14: Percentage of male (left) and female (right) mathematicians that continue publishing for another 1 to 10 years after having been active for 5 years. The colors indicate cohorts, with dark colors indicating the most recent ones. The figure exposes a "publishing drop-out rate" in mathematics throughout the past four decades.

In both plots the shrinkage of active researchers is evident and follows a linear decrease. This means that even after having been publishing for 5 years, academics do leave their field within their postdoctoral to early professor years. This is a known fact for which Figure 14 is able to offer deeper insights: thanks to the longitudinal analysis encoded in the color bar, it is apparent that mathematicians from earlier cohorts, i.e. those shown in lighter shades in both plots, remained in academia at a much larger rate than recent ones. This confirms that it has become progressively more difficult to secure a permanent position in mathematics. The increase in the number of graduate students that does not correlate with a parallel growth of tenured positions is certainly one of the causes of this development, as is the fact that an academic career is not any longer the only possible, or even desirable, outcome for mathematics (and in general for STEM) PhDs.

Another fact that immediately draws our attention is the discrepancy between the "publishing drop-out rates" for men (left) and women (right). Mainly, the percentage of female mathematicians that abandon academic research is larger than their male counterparts by a few percent points over a decade. Moreover, the longitudinal analysis shows that the increased drop-out rate for men has developed continuously over time, i.e. recent cohorts consistently display higher drop-out figures, evidenced by the clear ordering of the color shades. On the contrary, the evolution for women mathematicians does not follow such a clear chronological trend, as one can see lighter lines (older cohorts) at drop-out rates comparable to those of recent cohorts. The curves reflecting women's careers in academic research also exhibit a less smooth curvature. These features indicate that the permanence of women mathematicians in academia has suffered from factors other than the well-known increased difficulty in attaining a professorial rank in recent years; other various structural and systemic factors must have affected the careers of female mathematicians in ways different from those of men.

The productivity gap in mathematics

Women's underrepresentation in science has frequently been associated with the existence of a gender productivity gap that seems to be backed up by data on research output: several studies point out that women author fewer scientific papers, receive fewer grants and are not hired as often than men. This claim does not necessarily mean that male scientists outperform their female colleagues in absolute terms. Evidently, the amount of authored scientific papers does not categorically correlate with excellence in science. Indeed, there are many interacting sociological and cultural factors underlying the gender productivity gap (for a meta-analysis see [2]).

Science policy makers have already reacted and decided to counteract productivity measurements based solely on the amount of publications, e.g. the guidelines for the submission of project proposals to the Deutsche Forschungsgemeinschaft now require a maximum list of the ten most important publications per applicant. Nevertheless, the change in formalities has not yet permeated decision-making practices, thus committee members continue to take into account quantity over quality in their decisions. This raises the question of whether such practices are putting women at a disadvantage in their academic careers.

Below we examine the productivity of women and men in mathematics per number of years after career start. We consider only mathematicians that have published for at least 10 years. Additionally, we group them in academic cohorts in order to understand the longitudinal development of their productivity in relation to each other.

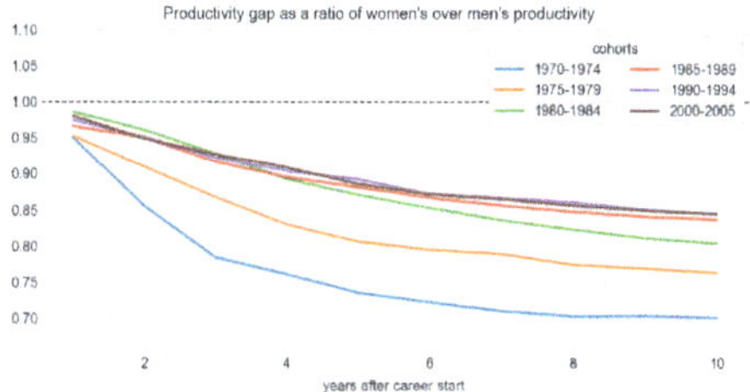

Figure 15: Ratio of publications from women mathematicians over men as a function of the years after career start.

Figure 15 displays the ratio of publications from female mathematicians over men as a function of the years after career start. Cohorts have been grouped in 5-year intervals. The gender productivity gap is evident for all cohorts and is specially noticeable in the first 4 years after the first publication. On a positive note, the gap has been closing since 1970, as evidenced by the less steep curves from recent years. However, progress seems to have stagnated, as no improvement is appreciated among cohorts posterior to 1985. Among the reasons commonly cited to explain this persistent gap is the idea that productivity may be affected by peer recognition and therefore by the scientific landscape. Another set of explanations have to do with socio-psychological and cultural factors related to the fact that women devote more time to teaching or administration and prioritize different aspects of their lives, which has been presented as personal career and lifestyle choices.

Figure 16 validates a repeatedly verified claim regarding the gender productivity gap, namely that the underrepresentation of women is more extreme as one considers more elite ranges of performance. The plot shows a histogram of the quotients of the median number of publications of women cohorts over men cohorts. Values have been computed for all cohorts at once. The predominance of the value 1 indicates that, in terms of the median,

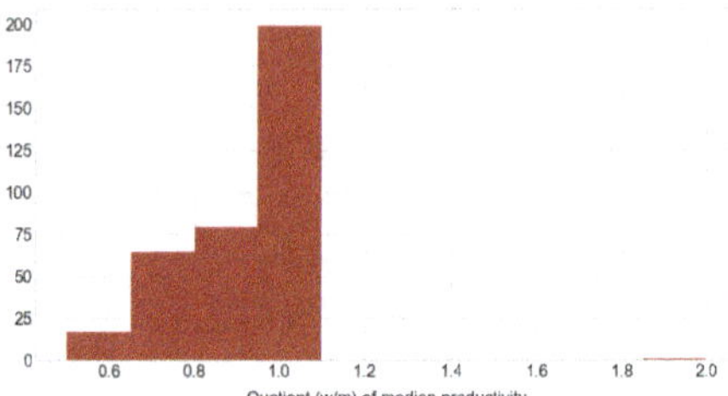

Figure 16: Histogram of the quotients of the median number of publications of women cohorts over men cohorts in mathematics.

women and men publish often as much. It is therefore the top performers, who are most frequently men, that primarily drive the productivity gap. Indeed, in mathematics, among all core mathematicians active for at least 10 years and with more than 100 publications, 5,496 are men and 237 are women. This result is in agreement with the thesis that individuals vary in research productivity predominantly because of the generative mechanism of incremental differentiation [1]. According to this theory, successful women researchers may need to over-accumulate, e.g., acquire more knowledge, build more relationships, work longer hours, to achieve the same level of increase in outputs as their male counterparts.

Situation of women in mathematics around the world

To round up the analysis of mathematicians per gender, we combine percentages of female mathematicians with geo-information extracted from all single-author papers in Core Math corresponding to the past 10 years. We choose to look at articles written individually to be able assess the importance of the contributions from women mathematicians regardless of coauthorship and collaboration dynamics. In the time period 2009-2018 the average share of single-author publications in Core Math that can be attributed to women is 10% of the total. We analyze their geographical distribution to unveil trends in different world regions.

Figure 17 (p. 112) provides a pristine picture of the situation of women in mathematics around the world, based on their single-authored research output in the Core Math in 2009-2018. Countries in grey are those for which not enough data was available. The map displays the *relative deviation from the average proportion* of single-author publications

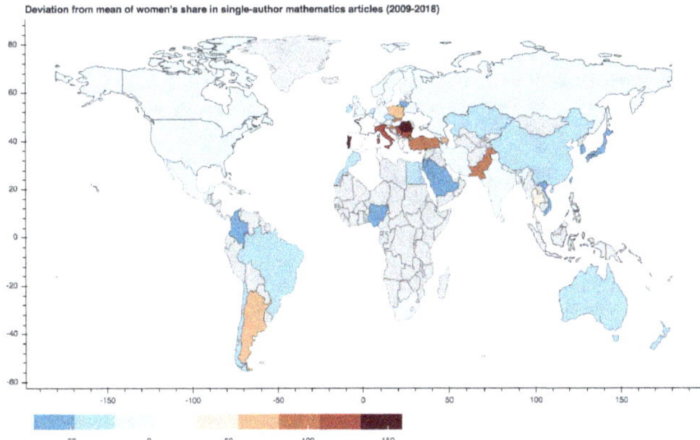

Figure 17: Relative deviation from the average proportion of women in single-author mathematics publications from zbMATH's Core Math data set in 2009-2018 broken down by the authors' countries of work.

in different countries. To illustrate this metric, let us consider the following example: say, women account for 8% of all single-authored papers published by scientists working in a given country C. Then the relative deviation from the mean, which in our case equals 10%, for country C would be 100*(8-10)/10 = -200/10 = -20, compared to the absolute deviation of -2%. The relative deviation from the mean thus helps to understand the differences in the context of the mean and, for instance, to compare the difference between 8% and an average of 10% to the difference between 92% and a group average of 90%.

For our choropleth maps this implies that in light blue areas we can expect to see quite precisely 10% of single-author papers to be written by women. Positive relative deviations from the mean are largest in countries from South- and East-Europe such as Portugal, Romania, Bulgaria, Serbia, and Italy, all of them featuring more than 20% women. On the other side, and apart from the grey-shadowed countries, the situation for women is worse in Nigeria, Lithuania, Vietnam, Jordan, Saudi Arabia, Colombia, and Japan, with dismal rates of female single authors below 5%. The reader should bear in mind that no data analysis of this kind can be completely exact, as incomplete and incorrect data from author profiles, assigned gender, and country extraction affects our statistics. Still, Figure 17 constitutes a valuable resource to identify trends and world regions regarding the participation of women in mathematics.

5 Astronomy and astrophysics

We present our analysis of the field of astronomy and astrophysics based on the data from ADS from 1970 to March 2018. We put special emphasis into characterizing the discipline and providing geo-specific information. We then expose our findings in relation to gender.

5.1 Methodology

Definition of core astronomy

Similar to zbMATH, ADS indexes a wide range of literature in astronomy and astrophysics, as well as in related sciences, most notably planetary sciences and solar physics. As a result, many individual works by authors working primarily in physics fields other than astrophysics can be found in the repository. In order to be able to limit the analysis scope to publications from researchers primarily focused on astronomy and astrophysics, an operational definition of core astronomy should be put in place.

Contrary to the MSC in mathematics, in ADS there is no fine-granular classification scheme for the publications that we could resort to in order to filter journals according to their relevance for astronomy and astrophysics. Upon analyzing the titles contained in the database, we implemented a simple method: we considered all serials containing "astro" in their name as core astronomy. The advantage of this straightforward approach is that it works in most languages, thus enabling a country-agnostic selection. Consequently, we considered every person who has published in a core astronomy journal, plus in Nature or Science (as long as indexed in ADS), to be an astronomer. In this way, we ensured a global selection of relevant research in astronomy and astrophysics, filtering out related areas outside the scope of our study.

In their quantitative analysis of gender bias in citations in astronomy and astrophysics literature, [4] restricted their analysis to the following five journals: The Astrophysical Journal, Astronomy and Astrophysics, Monthly Notices of the Royal Astronomical Society,

Nature and Science. Their argument that these "encompass the vast part of astronomical research today" is partially true: the first three serials already comprise a third of all publications indexed in ADS, in contrary to the more spread out situation in mathematics. However, for an inclusive study we preferred to consider a larger set of journals as core astronomy. This is based on the fact that among authors labeled as core astronomers with more than 4 publications over at least 3 years, almost 20% have never published in one of those 5 journals. This indicates that a subset of the contributors to astronomy and astrophysics research routinely submits to journals besides those considered in [4].

Data overview

We examined all publications indexed in ADS from 1970 until March 2018 authored by a core astronomer as defined in 5.1; we discarded miscellaneous publication types such as erratum, catalog, bookreview, abstract and obituary, which retains what is broadly considered original research contributions. This constitutes by far the largest part of the database. We considered 777,270 publications corresponding to 2,972,255 instances of authorships, yielding an average of 3.8 authors per article. Among these authorships, 1,775,771 (60%) were assigned to men, 317,628 (12%) to women, and 878,856 (28%) could not be assigned to any gender. Without the unknown, women accounted for 15% of all considered authorships.

The ADS does not offer author disambiguation, thus we applied our own algorithm as defined in 2.3 to cluster all authorships into individual researcher profiles. This procedure gave rise to 181,172 author profiles. We have applied our gender assignment algorithm as described in 2.5 to the constructed author profiles and were able to assign a gender to 93,608 (52%) of all of them; among those, 74,970 (80%) authors were classified as men and 18,638 (20%) as women.

It should be noted though that a very large proportion of the profiles with unknown gender contain a unique or a handful of publications, thus they either belong to students that later leave the field, or they could not be undoubtedly assigned to a larger profile by our algorithm due to name ambiguity. The level of name ambiguity is particularly high in the ADS due to the predominance of shortened initials instead of full names in the publications' metadata. Therefore one should bear in mind that our constructed author profiles might generally lack a few publications per researcher. However we see no reason to assume a significant gender bias as a consequence.

5.2 Results

General statistics

Below are the main discoveries from our analysis of astronomy and astrophysics publications indexed by the ADS. The most noteworthy change in the field has occurred in the number of authorships, that have grown by a ten-fold factor since 1970, reaching about 175,000 yearly in 2017. In comparison, the number of articles has only doubled in the same amount of time, approaching 25,000 per year in the present decade. Astronomy and astrophysics has progressively become more of a "big science" discipline, characterized by large scientific teams and partner collaborations that carry on substantial projects, often tied to massive research facilities such as telescopes and astronomic observatories. Figure 18 displays the comparably larger gap that has been opening between the number of articles and the number of authorships. The contrast with the equivalent picture for mathematics in Figure 3 (p. 99) is unmistakable.

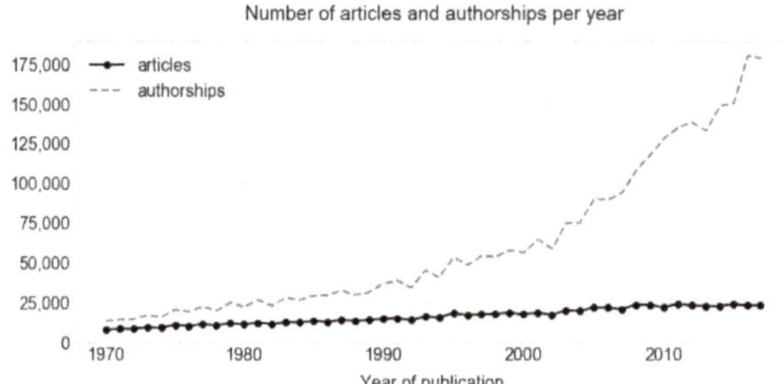

Figure 18: Number of published articles and corresponding authorships per year in astronomy and astrophysics as indexed by ADS.

As mentioned in 2.2, publications with multiple authors are the norm in astronomy and astrophysics, much more than in other fields like mathematics or computer science. Figure 19 (p. 116) sheds light on the evolution of the number of authors per paper over time.

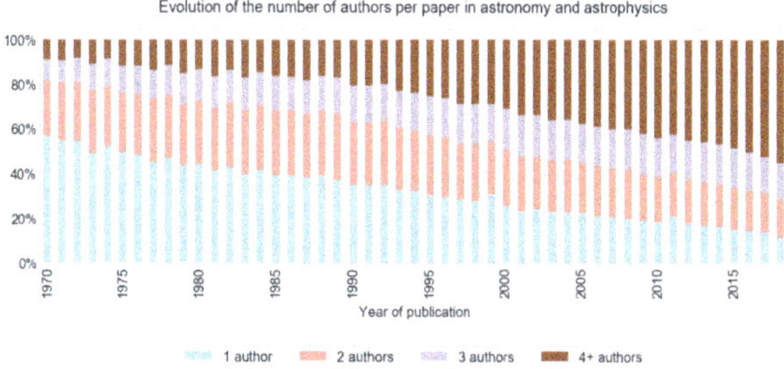

Figure 19: Evolution of the number of authors per paper in astronomy and astrophysics since 1970.

In 1970 approximately 60% of all published papers were written by one or two authors. The situation has profoundly changed within the past decades: currently about 55% of all papers in astronomy and astrophysics have more than three authors, hinting at an extremely collaborative field. It is certainly interesting to note that the size of the working groups where scientists are embedded ought to exert an influence on gender dynamics therein. Maybe not so coincidentally, the situation of women in astronomy and astrophysics in regards to publications in top journals has been shown to be more positive than in other disciplines that favor more individual work. One could thus conclude that more open environments seem to foster the development of women's careers.

Gender analysis in astronomy and astrophysics

Active female astronomers

Using author profiles from the ADS records that could be reasonably disambiguated and assigned a gender, Figure 20 displays the number of active (publishing) astronomers since 1970 and the percentage of them that are women. Although the number of authorships in astronomy and astrophysics has skyrocketed in recent decades, as shown in 5.2, the number of researchers publishing in the field has increased in a much more controlled way. This is a consequence of the above mentioned tremendous rise of publications with sizable author lists, which blows up the total number of authorships.

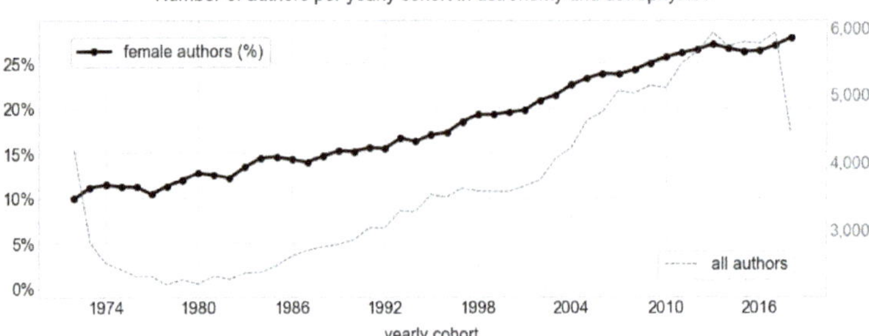

Figure 20: Number of active (publishing) astronomers since 1970 and percentage of them that are women.

The proportion of women in astronomy and astrophysics over the past decades has followed a similar evolution to that in mathematics: from figures in the range of 10% in 1970, the percentage has doubled within the past five decades. Yet from the analysis of top journals in both disciplines we could assess that the presence of women in astronomy and astrophysics journals is larger than in mathematics (see Figures 39 and 42). A major difference in publication dynamics among both fields is the average number of authors per paper, as we have seen. We can thus again conclude that the more cooperative environment enjoyed by astronomers and the larger collaborations in which they partake might be conducive to more positive career outcomes in astronomy and astrophysics in comparison with mathematics.

Career length of men and women in astronomy and astrophysics

Figure 21 (p. 118) shows, for cohorts from 1970 until 2003, the share of men (left) and women (right) who are active for another 1 to 10 years after having published academic articles in astronomy and astrophysics for five years. We have applied window smoothing to get a cleaner picture of the displayed data. The picture is similar to what was seen for mathematics in Figure 14 (p. 108): cohorts of astronomers leave academia at an approximately linear rate over the decade starting 5 years after their first publication. This decline has progressively become steeper in recent years, due to increased difficulty in securing a permanent position in astronomy and astrophysics. Roughly speaking, an astronomer that published their first paper in 2000 will have left academia in 2015 with a 50% probability. Finally, focusing on the differences between women and men, we see two main features. Firstly, the drop-out rates of female astronomer are more scattered than those of their male counterparts. Secondly, analogous as in mathematics, it is apparent that the evolution of the average drop-out rate in astronomy and astrophysics for women over the years does not completely follow the clear tendency exhibited by men's.

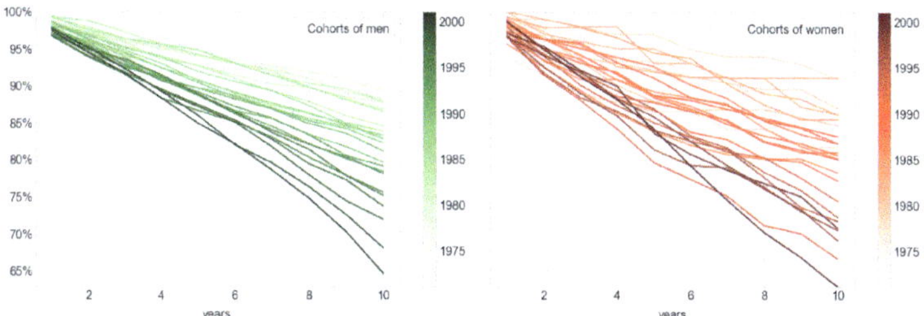

Figure 21: Percentage of male (left) and female (right) astronomers that continue publishing for another 1 to 10 years after having been active for five years. This exposes the drop-out rate in astronomy and astrophysics throughout the past four decades.

The productivity gap in astronomy and astrophysics

We next present an analysis of the gender productivity gap in astronomy and astrophysics. We consider only astronomers that have published for at least 10 years. Additionally, we group them in academic cohorts in order to understand the longitudinal development of their productivity in relation to each other. Figure 22 displays the ratio of publications from female astronomers over men as a function of the years after career start. Cohorts have been grouped in 5-year intervals. A pronounced gender gap is appreciated for the cohorts from the early 1970s, when women merely published 75% of their fellow male astronomers' research. In subsequent years, the gap has clearly closed, such that more recent cohorts of women and men publish comparable number of articles within a 10% difference. This is a positive and very welcomed development.

The question of the distribution of publications per astronomers, i.e. the impact of 'superstars', or top performers, is analyzed in Figure 23. We compute the ratio of the median number of publications from women and men and display results as a histogram. The

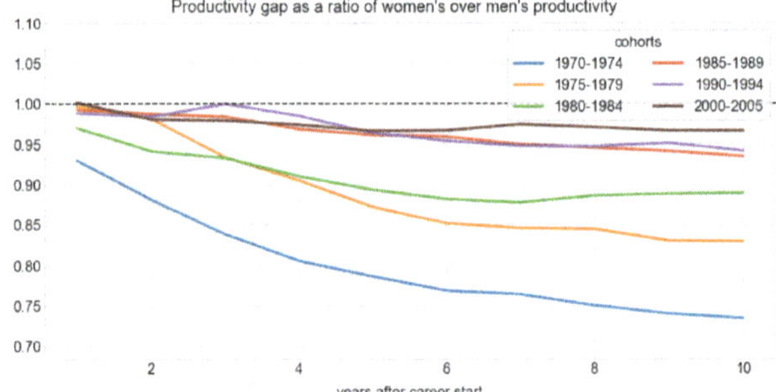

Figure 22: Ratio of publications from women astronomers over men as a function of the years after career start.

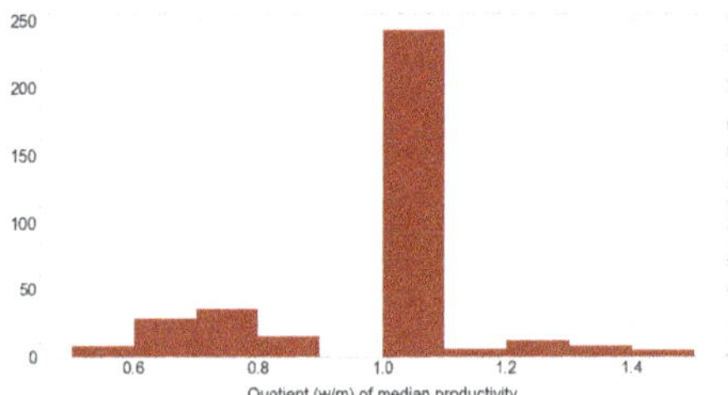

Figure 23: Histogram of the quotients of the median number of publications of women over men in astronomy and astrophysics.

resulting distribution is strongly centered around the value 1.0, confirming that differences in productivity from standard performers are not severe. Again the contributions of authors at the top percentiles of the distribution greatly contribute to the existence of the productivity gap.

For a field like astronomy and astrophysics, where, as we know, typical publications contain multiple authors, first-author papers are especially important to build an independent career. Therefore we present below a similar productivity analysis as above, but restricted to the authorships at position one. Figure 24 (p. 120) indicates a similar picture as before but with a clearer difference between the cohorts after 1985.

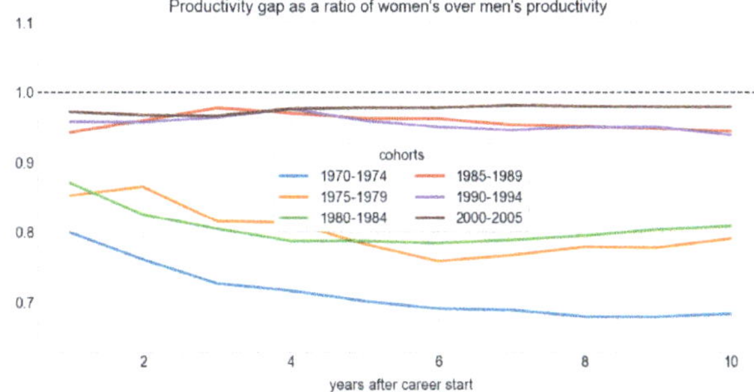

Figure 24: Ratio of first-author publications from women astronomers over men as a function of the years after career start.

Situation of women in astronomy and astrophysics around the world

We finalize the analysis of the field of astronomy and astrophysics in relation to gender by combining female participation statistics with country-level information.

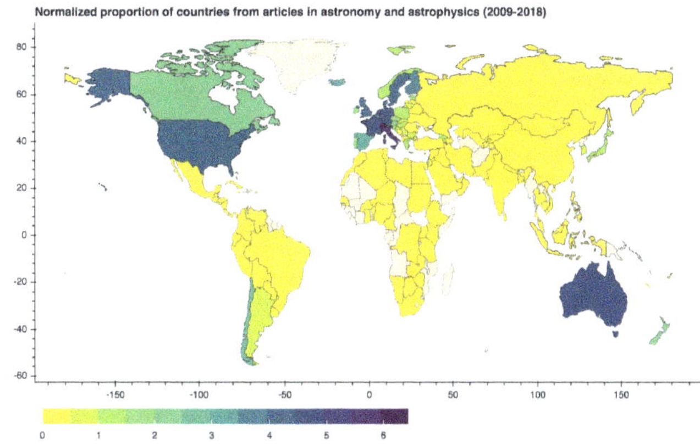

Figure 25: Proportion of countries of work from astronomers based on articles in ADS from 2009-2018, normalized by the average population size in the respective country in the same period of time.

In contrast to zbMATH, the majority of the data in ADS has affiliations on the level of authorships. This allows us to visualize the geographical distribution of astronomers and astrophysicists without having to limit ourselves to articles with only one author, as we did for mathematics. To ensure the best possible comparability with mathematics, we have looked at publications from 2009 to 2018. The chropleth map in Figure 25 shows the geographical distribution, normalized by averaged country population size during that time. Over the last 10 years, most of the research in this field has been carried out in the USA and Europe. Among the European countries, Italy stands out particularly, followed by Germany, France and the Netherlands. Unlike in mathematics, China and Russia seem to play a rather minor role in astronomy and astrophysics. In the South American continent Chile takes a stronger part, followed by Argentina. Similar to mathematics, however, the majority of Africa is hardly represented.

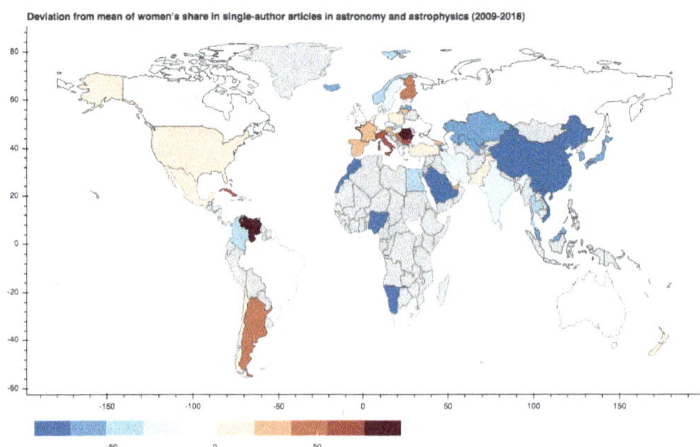

Figure 26: Deviation from the average proportion of women in single-author astronomy and astrophysics publications from ADS broken down by the authors' countries of work.

Figure 26 gives an overview of the geographical distribution of female astronomers based on their publications in ADS. Countries in grey are those for which not enough data was available. The map displays the deviation from the average proportion in different countries, i.e. in light blue areas we can expect to see exactly 13.4% of papers to be written by women. Positive deviations from the mean are largest in Venezuela, Romania, Bulgaria, Italy, Finland, Argentina, and Cuba, all of them featuring 20% to 25% women. On the other side, and apart from the grey-shadowed countries, the situation for women is worse in China, Saudi Arabia, Nigeria, Morocco, Western Sahara, and Namibia, with dismal rates of female single authors below 2%. The reader should bear in mind that no data analysis of this kind can be completely exact, as incomplete and incorrect data from author profiles, assigned gender, and country extraction affects our statistics. Still, Figure 26 constitutes a valuable resource to identify trends and world regions regarding the participation of women in astronomy and astrophysics.

6 Theoretical physics

We present our analysis of the field of theoretical physics based on the data from the arXiv from 1991 to July 2019. We put special emphasis into characterizing the discipline but due to missing affiliations we can not provide geo-specific information. We then expose our findings in relation to gender.

6.1 Methodology

Data overview

Contrary to the analyses in mathematics and astronomy and astrophysics, where the existence of curated and field-specific databases zbMATH and ADS respectively ensures access to a comprehensive and mostly complete corpus of bibliometric metadata, in the case of theoretical physics no comparable repository exists. Admittedly, the high energy physics (HEP) community maintains a dedicated platform, the INSPIRE information system[19], that programmatically harvests content from other bibliographic resources that reliably publish high-quality content in relevant areas. Those sources include, but are not restricted to, arXiv e-prints from hep*, gr-qc, nucl*, astro-ph.CO, astro-ph.HE, physics.acc-ph, physics.data-an and physics.ins-det archives. In addition, conference contributions, theses, technical reports and experimental notes are also added to the database.

---

[19]`http://inspirehep.net/`

When pondering the most suitable repository to query a comprehensive and curated collection of relevant articles in theoretical physics, not only in HEP, we took into consideration the fact that standard publication practices from physicists, especially in theoretical subfields, routinely comprise uploading preprints to the arXiv. In fact, it is so common that in fields like HEP, many peer-reviewed journals allow submission of papers from arXiv directly, using the arXiv e-print number. This preprint repository is "an indispensable mode of scientific exchange" [9] in particular in physics, "covering the majority of publications in subfields like astronomy, astrophysics, and nuclear and particle physics" [13]. The use in other disciplines is continuously increasing. Preprints are enriched a posteriori with publication metadata once they are accepted, which renders the arXiv a very interesting data source for the purpose of studying publication dynamics.

We have implemented a mechanism to perform continuous updates of the arXiv repository. We analyzed the full collection of data indexed in the arXiv from its beginnings in the early 1990s. Among all available arXiv subcategories, we selected those relevant for theoretical physics, namely Astrophysics, Condensed Matter, General Relativity and Quantum Cosmology, High Energy Physics, Mathematical Physics, Nonlinear Sciences, Nuclear Experiment, Nuclear Theory, Physics (General) and Quantum Physics. For entries with multiple categories, we considered the first one as principal. This corresponds to the current and old arXiv categories cond-mat, physics, astro-, nlin, nucl, hep-, gr-qc, quant, acc-phys, adap-org, ao-sci, atom-ph, bayes-an, chao-dyn, chem-ph, comp-gas, mtrl-th, patt-sol, plasm-ph, solv-int, supr-cond. The data set comprises 1,667,512 documents corresponding to 4,505,508 instances of authorship, yielding an average of 2.7 authors per article. The arXiv does not offer author disambiguation, thus we applied our own algorithm to cluster all authorships into individual researcher profiles. This procedure gave rise to 458,485 author profiles. We have applied our gender assignment algorithm as described in 2.5 to the constructed author profiles and were able to assign a gender to 281,602 (61%) of all of them; among those, 47,075 (17%) authors were classified as women and 234,527 (83%) as men.

6.2 Results

General statistics

We present the findings of our analyses of the arXiv focused on theoretical physics. Figure 27 illustrates the evolution of the number of preprints uploaded to the service since the early 1990s. What started as a dedicated repository for physics research has expanded to accommodate other STEM disciplines. However, even today, physics preprints make up for about half of all uploaded content. The service is currently indexing way above 100,000 documents per year and about 60,000 of them belong to physics, which we will concentrate on. Figure 28 (p. 125) displays the break-down per physics subfields. The initial preponderance of high energy physics has given rise to a quite balanced distribution nowadays, as the usage of the arXiv has become standard practice for physicists of other disciplines as well.

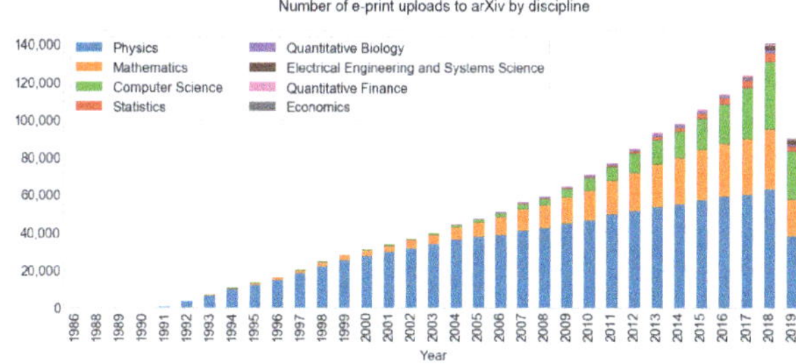

Figure 27: Number of preprints indexed by the arXiv per year broken down by main discipline.

Analogous to our analysis of mathematics and astronomy and astrophysics, we investigate next the level of collaboration in the theoretical physics domain by looking at the distribution and evolution of the number of authors per paper. In Figure 29 we display the chrononological progression of publications with 1, 2, 3, and more authors in all indexed arXiv physics preprints. Articles with more than 3 authors represented less than 10% of the total when the arXiv started operating in 1991. That figure has grown to reach almost half of all current physics preprints, following the same trend that could be seen in Figures 4 and 19 for other STEM disciplines.

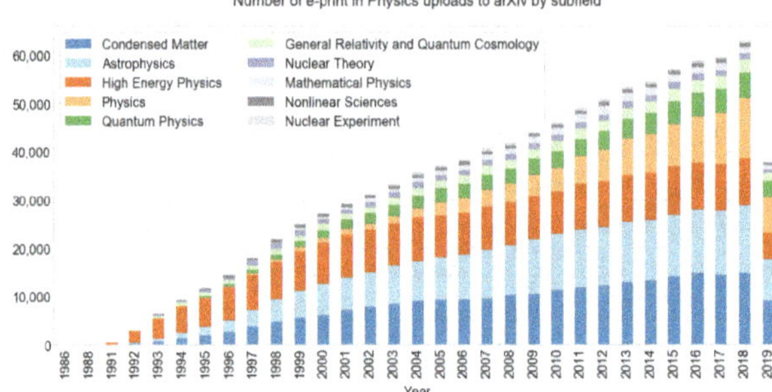

Figure 28: Number of physics preprints indexed by the arXiv per year broken down by subfield.

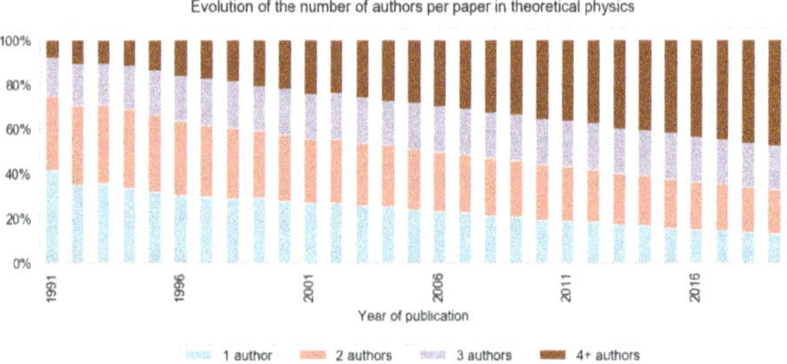

Figure 29: Evolution of the number of authors per paper in theoretical physics as indexed in the arXiv since 1991.

This evidences that physics is also evolving in the direction of "big science" where research is conducted within large, mostly international collaborations. This is a well-known trend in high energy physics, due to the magnitude of the experimental machinery needed to push the frontiers of knowledge in elementary particle physics. However, we would like to investigate whether other physics subfields are also characterized by substantial cooperation, and in that case, which disciplines exhibit said behaviour most prominently.

To aid in the visualization of collaborative trends in the different subdisciplines, we first focus on single-author publications. Figure 30 (p. 126) displays the evolution of their percentages labeled by its corresponding research area. From the plot we have removed the

3 smallest subfields observed in Figure 28, namely Nuclear Theory, Nuclear Experiment, and Nonlinear Sciences, as they exhibit statistics too small to offer robust conclusions. In all subfields the same tendency towards a reduction on the preponderance of single-author publications is observed, with current percentages ranging from 10% to 30% of the total of preprints per year. Nevertheless, some fields are notoriously more collaborative than others: the percentage of single-author papers is the smallest in Condensed Physics and Astrophysics, reaching values under 10% in recent years. Perhaps somehow surprisingly, in High Energy Physics over 20% of all preprints are written solo, placing the subfield in an intermediate position between the already mentioned most collaborative areas and the more individually-focused Mathematical Physics.

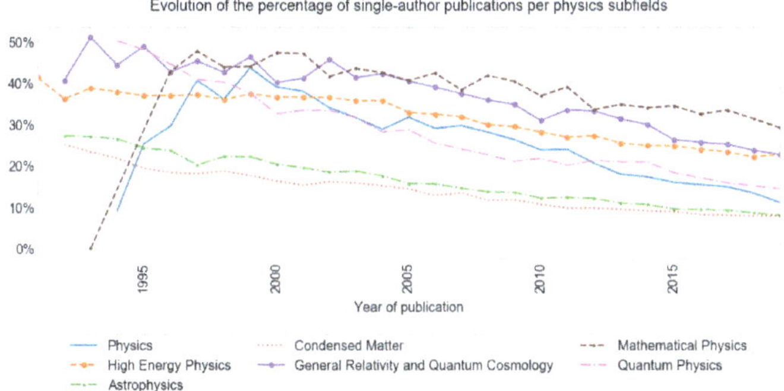

Figure 30: Evolution of the percentage of single-author publications in theoretical physics as indexed in the arXiv since 1991.

To complement the insights from single-author preprints, we take a look at publications authored by 4 or more researchers, displayed in Figure 31. The proportion of said multi-author research publications has consistently grown in all analyzed subfields over the past 30 years. Notably aside from collaborative publishing trends are Mathematical Physics and to a certain extent General Relativity and Quantum Cosmology, both areas characterized by their heavy mathematical focus. This validates the known trends observed in the analysis of mathematics in 4.2. On the other side of the spectrum, highly collaborative fields where multi-author publications represent about half of the total are Astrophysics, confirming our findings from 5.2, and Condensed Matter.

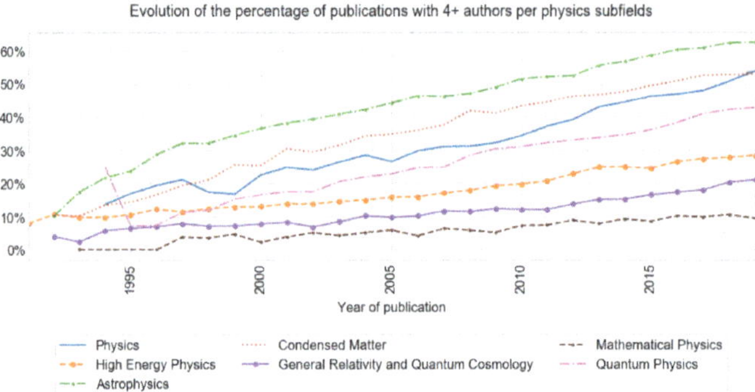

Figure 31: Evolution of the number of publications with more than 3 authors in theoretical physics as indexed in the arXiv since 1991.

Gender analysis in theoretical physics

Female presence in theoretical physics

Physics has traditionally been viewed as one of the most masculine of the scientific fields, a discipline in which women are regarded as unfit or uninterested to participate. In the last 150 years since Marie Curie won her Nobel Prize in physics, only two other women have received this accolade: Maria Goeppert-Mayer in 1965 and Donna Strickland in 2018. An analysis of the arXiv and its indexed publications in physics for the past 30 years can serve as a proxy of the situation of female physicists in recent times.

Using author profiles from the arXiv physics preprints that could be reasonably disambiguated and assigned a gender, Figure 32 (p. 128) displays the number of active (publishing) physicists since 1970 and the percentage of them that are women. Currently, approximately 30,000 authors appear yearly in the arXiv, a number that has continuously grown since the beginnings of the service in the early 1990s. The percentage of them that are women has increased over the past 30 years from the upper single digits to about 20% nowadays. This welcomed improvement is nevertheless not enough to bring the situation of women in physics on par with that in astronomy and mathematics. The comparison among Figures 13 (p. 107), 20 (p. 117), and 32 clearly prompts the observation that, although all three analyzed disciplines mathematics, astronomy and astrophysics, and theoretical physics have seen major advances over the past decades regarding women participation, the latter remains as the least gender diverse of the three.

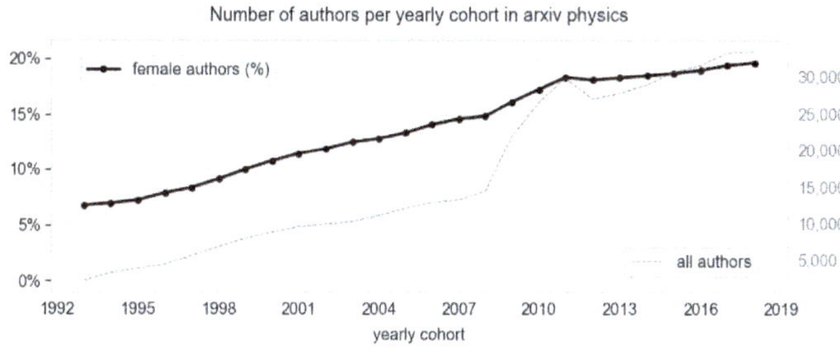

Figure 32: Number of active (publishing) physicists and percentage of them that are women.

Making use of the arXiv subcategories, let us know have a look at gender statistics by physics disciplines. Figure 33 (p. 129) displays the percentage of authorships by women in the selected physics subfields indexed by the arXiv in 2009-2019. All preprints in high energy physics (Experiment, Lattice, Phenomenology, and Theory) have been aggregated together. The most noticeable fact is the outlier status of astrophysics: whereas all other physics subfields exhibit female percentages ranging from 6% to 9%, astrophysics practically doubles that figure.

It is a known fact that astronomy and astrophysics have a long history of involving women. Already in the late 1800s some observatories hired women to examine thousands of photographs to calculate stars' positions and analyze their spectra. Employees were expected to perform involved calculations, yet women were given positions with relatively low status and pay. Regardless, this early involvement of women in astronomy and related fields is probably at the root of the relatively better current stand of female astrophysicists with respect to their physics counterparts.

Figure 34 offers a glimpse into the chronological evolution of the different subfields in theoretical physics. As already mentioned, historical reasons are possibly at the core of

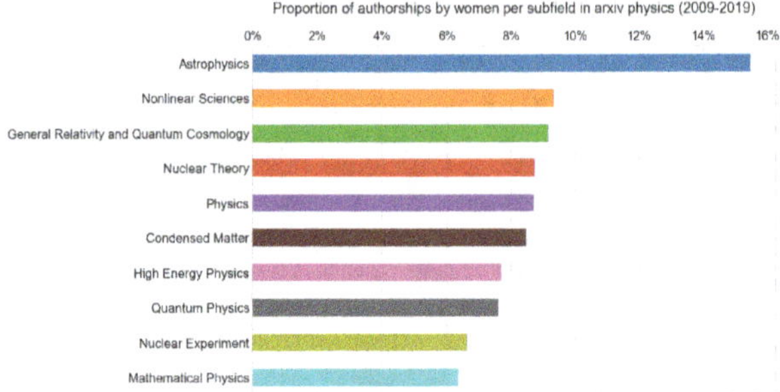

Figure 33: Proportion of authorships by women per physics subfields in publications indexed in the arXiv in 2009-2019. High Energy Physics includes subcategories Experiment, Lattice, Phenomenology, and Theory.

why astrophysics is an immediately recognizable (positive) outlier. Yet, despite showing percentages of women's participation that double those of other physics subfields, a certain decelerated growth seems to be affecting astrophysics in the current decade, the percentage of female authorships having stagnated at around 15% in recent years. In fact, a timely report on the status of women in physics and astronomy indicates that, "while the number of women earning astronomy degrees has steadily increased between 2007-2017, the number of men earning degrees has shown greater increases. Therefore, the total percentage of women earning astronomy bachelor's degrees has decreased in recent years (33% in 2017 compared to 40% in 2007)" [19]. Further evolution of the field will need to be monitored to confirm whether the positive trend enjoyed by astrophysics regarding female enrollment gets reversed or not.

All remaining physics subfields see a positive evolution in the percentages of females, with figures ranging from below 5% in the early 1990s to the current situation featuring about 8-10%. No major differences in magnitude among subfields are appreciated, the most interesting insight perhaps being the flatter curves in high energy and quantum physics that seem to have also reached a plateau in the past decade. Neither fields have traditionally been at the forefront of gender awareness: only recently there seems to be an awoken interest in fostering discussion on the interplay of high energy physics and gender, with several workshops and conferences being organized at several institutions, most notaby CERN.

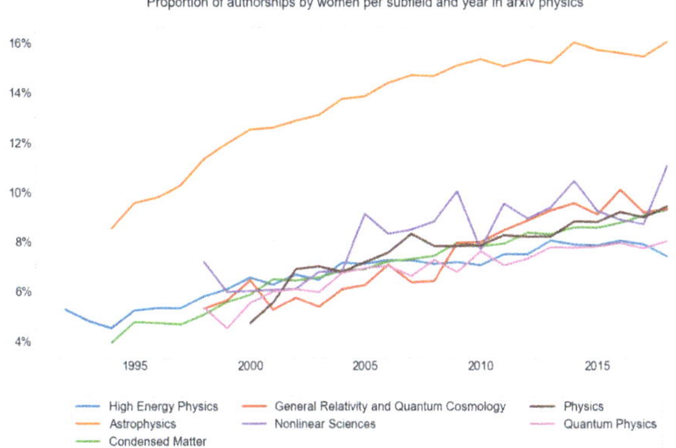

Figure 34: Proportion of authorships by women per physics subfields and year in publications indexed in the arXiv.

Career length of men and women in theoretical physics

Although data gathered from the arXiv corresponds to the last 30 years rather than the last 50 provided by zbMATH and ADS, it is possible to produce a similar analysis about the career length and dropout likelihood in physics based on the amount of uploaded preprints. In Figure 35 we show for cohorts from 1996 until 2001, the share of men (left) and women (right) who are active for another 1 to 10 years after contributing preprints to the physics arXiv for 5 years. We apply window smoothing to get a cleaner picture of the displayed data. The picture is similar that for mathematics and astronomy and astrophysics in Figures 14 (p. 108) and 21 (p. 118): cohorts of physicists leave academia at an approximately linear rate over the decade starting 5 years after their first publication. All conclusions reached for the other two analyzed disciplines hold for physics as well. Therefore we can conclude that the observed trends regarding career length and dropout prospects for both men and women researchers can be extrapolated to most STEM fields.

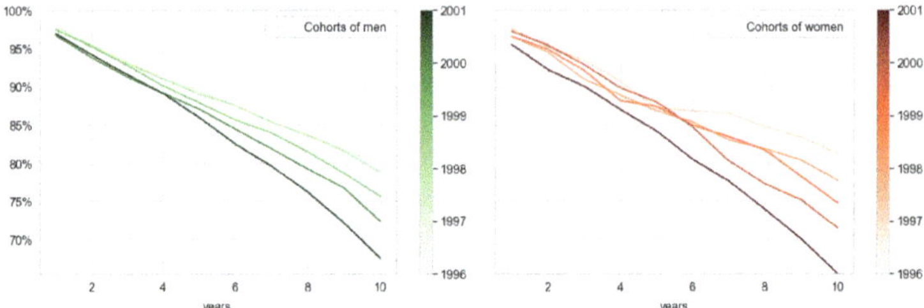

Figure 35: Percentage of male (left) and female (right) physicists that continue publishing for another 1 to 10 years after having been active for five years. This exposes the drop-out rate in physics for 5 cohorts from 1996 until 2001.

The productivity gap in theoretical physics

Finally, we analyze the gender productivity gap in theoretical physics. We group authors by their academic cohorts in order to understand the longitudinal development of their productivity in relation to each other.

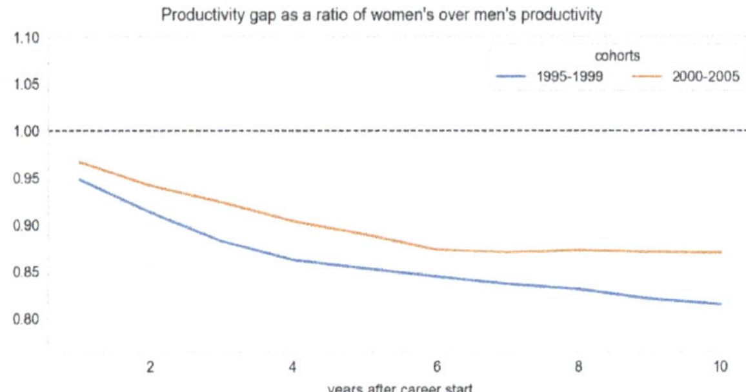

Figure 36: Ratio of publications from women physicists over men as a function of the years after career start.

Figure 36 displays the ratio of publications from female astronomers over men as a function of the years after career start. Cohorts have been grouped in 5-year intervals; given the reduced amount of operating years of the arXiv, only two sets of aggregated cohorts could be built. The accompanying Figure 37 (p. 132) shows the histogram of the quotients

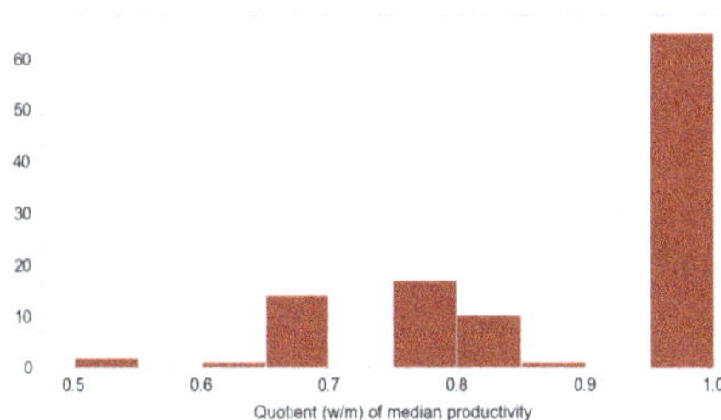

Figure 37: Histogram of the quotients of the median number of publications of women over men in physics.

of the median number of publications of women over men. Values have been computed for all cohorts at once. Analogous results to those in astronomy and astrophysics can be observed in both cases. However, the limited longitudinal data available makes it difficult to extrapolate to larger time periods. In any case, the same tendency towards a reduction of the gender productivity gap can be seen, which confirms again the positive trend towards comparable research outcomes from male and women researchers in terms of number of publications.

7 Publication in top journals and gendered trends

7.1 Assessing quality: journal rankings

Initially established with the purpose of communicating knowledge, promoting exchange of ideas, and advancing science, scholarly journals have also become an important vehicle for the forging of academic careers in STEM, as decisions on tenure, funding, and promotions strongly depend on a researcher's publication record. Moreover, it is not just the *number* of articles a scientist writes that matters, but also the *venue* where they appear. Publishing in highly renowned journals in one's discipline is a powerful determinant of tenure in many STEM fields including mathematics and physics, and an important predictor of professional success. Thus, any study on publication practices ought to take into account their impact in the making of academic careers. Regarding quality assessment, it can't be ignored that journal rankings are widely employed to measure prestige associated with publishing in one or another. Given its importance for academic careers as well as for the development of science policies, our analyses need to be able to distinguish among journals and, to a certain extent, to categorize them.

Plenty of bibliometric measures on the journal level, primarily based on citations, have been proposed that can be used as surrogates for quality. The most widespread is perhaps the Impact Factor (IF), with the Eigenfactor and the h-index as known alternatives. The interest in this kind of metrics arises from the fact that a journal ranking scheme might help elucidate the question whether publication practices, gender, and journal quality correlate in any sense. In fact, we showed in [16] that female mathematicians are underrepresented in publications on high-ranked mathematics journals, defined as those at the top of the IF and ERA (Excellence in Research for Australia) indicators. This result prompted interest to deepen the analyses, potentially extending them to other STEM fields.

Yet, regardless of the importance of having a reliable categorization to assess quality, it is by no means clear that journal rankings can provide said information meaningfully. Against the IF and similar ranking schemes a number of well-argued critiques has been formulated on the basis of technical issues, such as their concrete definition and implementation, or of interpretative concerns. For a deeper discussion of the use of journal rankings in assessing the quality of individual research, see e.g. [0, 12, 18, 10]. A consensus seems to be emerging that research quality shall not be measured based just on the one-dimensional scale of a journal ranking. We will therefore avoid applying any such ranking scheme in our analyses and will resort to expert domain knowledge to classify, select, and prioritize some journals above others. It is in this sense that we will refer to prominent journals as "top journals".

7.2 Self-reported publication practices: perceptions on submission to top journals

Prior to analyzing data from publications in top journals, it is important to investigate whether potential disparities in their publishing rates are originated already before the submission stage. A key question in the global survey of scientists in this regard was: *"During the last five years, how many articles have you submitted to journals that are top-ranked in your field?"* This question was intended to unveil trends in the publication habits of women and men. Respondents were asked to provide a number between 0 and 30 (larger values being joint together with 30).

In our analysis we have restricted to those respondents who (a) gave a numerical answer to the question[20], (b) hold at least a Master's or a Doctorate degree, and (c) selected one of the following six disciplines as their primary field, for which at least 1,000 answers were collected: 'Physics', 'Mathematics', 'Astronomy', 'Computer Science and Technology', 'Biological and Related Sciences' and 'Chemistry'. Among these 14,557 respondents were 7,767 men, 6,613 women and 177 individuals who preferred not to state their gender.

The majority of responses quoted a rather low number: the median is 3 submissions in the last 5 years for both women and men. The mean values in all three groups were very much alike, with 5,83 for women, 6,29 for men and 6,68 in the group that did not state their gender. Figure 38 (p. 134) displays answers as a histogram split by responses from women and men. Note that the peaks at multiples of 5 most likely indicate a rounding effect on the respondents' side. Both distributions are similar, with a slightly higher presence of women submitting between 1 and 4 articles to top journals, and a higher proportion of men in the long tail but also among those who stated that they have not submitted any article to a top journal.

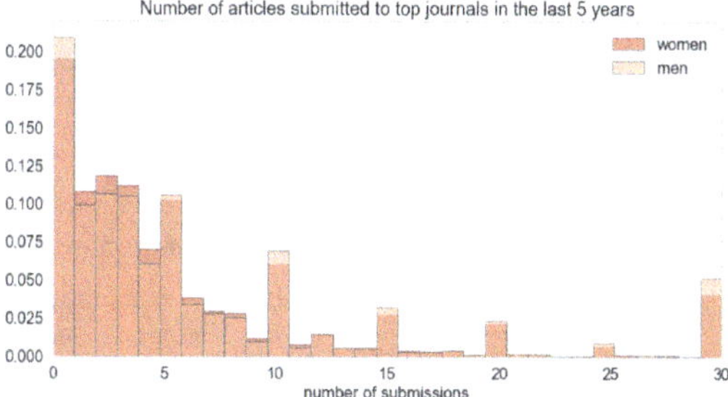

Figure 38: Histogram of the number of publications submitted to top journals in the last 5 years as self-reported by the respondents to the global survey's question *"During the last five years, how many articles have you submitted to journals that are top-ranked in your field?"* Dark (light) bars encode answers from women (men).

---

[20]Respondents had also the possibility to skip the question

We have computed test statistics to test the null hypothesis that there is no statistical difference between the self-reported submission rates of women and men. For this purpose we use the non-parametric Mann-Whitney U test, which computes two so-called "rank scores", i.e. the number of times a score from group 1 precedes in rank order a score from group 2, and vice versa (controlling for the minimal possible value for the rank sum) and is appropriate to decide whether two data sets have been sampled from populations having the same distribution. The test is applied to the following data sets: (1) total answers of all women and all men; (2) answers subdivided by discipline; (3) answers subdivided by world region. We set a significance level $\alpha = 0.05$ and apply the Bonferroni correction, yielding $\alpha \sim 0.008$ for the subgroup analysis (2) and $\alpha \sim 0.004$ in case (3), respectively.

For (1) we have gathered the responses of all women (6,613) compared to those of all men (7,767). The null hypothesis is rejected on this data set, meaning that it is inferred that men have submitted significantly more ($p < 0.04$) articles to top journals in the last 5 years. Although the difference is statistically significant, the effect size in terms of the the Rank-Biserial correlation[21] is almost negligible.

Regarding the grouped tests, the hypothesis was rejected only for the comparisons within world regions, namely South America and Northern Europe, however again with small effect sizes.

We deduce that even though we can statistically measure a difference between the self-reported submission numbers from women and men, with larger figures from the latter, its efect size is small. When broken down by region or discipline, we found basically no noteworthy differences.

To complete the picture we have built a multivariate linear model using an ordinary least squares (OLS) fit to predict the number of articles submitted to renowned journals in the last five years (the target variable) taking the following attributes as independent variables[22]:

---

[21] Said correlation equals the difference of the proportions of the two rank sums, where the proportion is meant with respect to the number of all possible comparisons between group 1 and 2. This indicator has a maximum value of 1, in which case in all pairwise comparisons between both groups the score of one of them would be smaller than the other's. A correlation value close to 0, on the other hand, implies that the effect is very small, as is the case.

[22] We have preprocessed the data by removing rows with missing values, replacing rare countries by a dummy value and transforming the target value with a logarithmic function in order to get as close as possible to preassumptions required for linear regression.

- highest academic degree (Masters/Doctoral)

- primary discipline (astronomy/physics/mathematics/chemistry/computer science/biology)

- gender (Female/Male/Prefer not to respond)

- age

- country

- parent or guardian of children (Yes/No)

- number of total/succesful grant applications in the last 5 years

- participation in 14 types of academic activities (e.g. journal editor, supervision of graduate students, etc.)

The model is overall significant, yielding an adjusted R^2 value of 0.42, meaning that the model explains around 42% of the variation in the data. We consider this a satisfactory overall result since our data clearly lacks important predictors such as the affiliated institution, type of position, teaching load or what exactly is meant by a renowned journal. We can look at the model's coefficients to estimate the effect of gender on the number of submitted articles while controlling for the other predictors. As suggested by the previous explorations, the effect of gender is rather small, with an increase of around 5%, when the gender is changed form women to men, while controlling for the other predictors. In contrast, the respondents' field of expertise has a much greater impact. When controlling for the other variables, submission numbers of astronomers are predicted to be significantly higher than those of researchers in the other five discipline. Compared to mathematicians for instance, respondents working in astronomy report to submit about 50% more to what they consider top journals. A higher effect on the target variable stems from factors such as the respondent's country or the participation in academic activities such as speaking at conferences or being a journal editor.

The next section will show real data from selected top journals to try to establish a meaningful comparison between self-reported submission rates and actual publication statistics.

7.3 Analysis of distributions in renowned journals

Regardless of the self-reported publication practices, we can study the distribution of authorships and gender from publications in each field's selected top journals. Combined with the above survey results, the obtained insights offer a clearer picture with concrete statistics for the representation of both genders in prominent publication venues. Below we display data from selected journals grouped by disciplines. In all figures, dots represent the percentage of fractional authorships attributed to women among all authorships with inferred gender, i.e. after removing unknown gender assignments. Solid curves are the result of fitting a locally weighted scatterplot smoothing regression (LOWESS) model to the data.

Mathematics

During the 19th century, in the course of the professionalization of mathematics, numerous national mathematical societies were formed, the oldest being the Moscow Mathematical Society, founded in 1864 [6, p. 73]. Similar to the educational institutions, the societies soon established their own journals, in which some of the most profound works of the discipline are still published today. We have thus decided to consider 18 renowned mathematical journals, nine of which are (co-)published by national societies. The other nine journals are particularly favored in certain subfields of mathematics and can be used as a proxy for what is considered high quality research in those areas.

Figure 39 (p. 138) displays the percentage of fractional authorships from women in top mathematics journal since 1970. In all considered serials the percentage of authorships from women since 1970 is predominantly constrained below 20%. A solid half of the society journals displayed on the left column show a positive trend. The bulletin of the French Mathematical Society shows a rather noisy behaviour and no clear chronological trend, with proportions of women ranging between almost 0 and over 20%. The average share is around 10%, similar to the Journal of the European Mathematical Society. The lowest figure is found in the Journal of the American Mathematical Society, where the proportion of women is around 5% or less, with no visible positive trend. The topical journals in the right column are arranged approximately after the MSC 2010. The last three journals, featuring rather work in areas of applied mathematics, show a rising development over time with shares above 10% in recent years. With the exception of the Journal of Differential

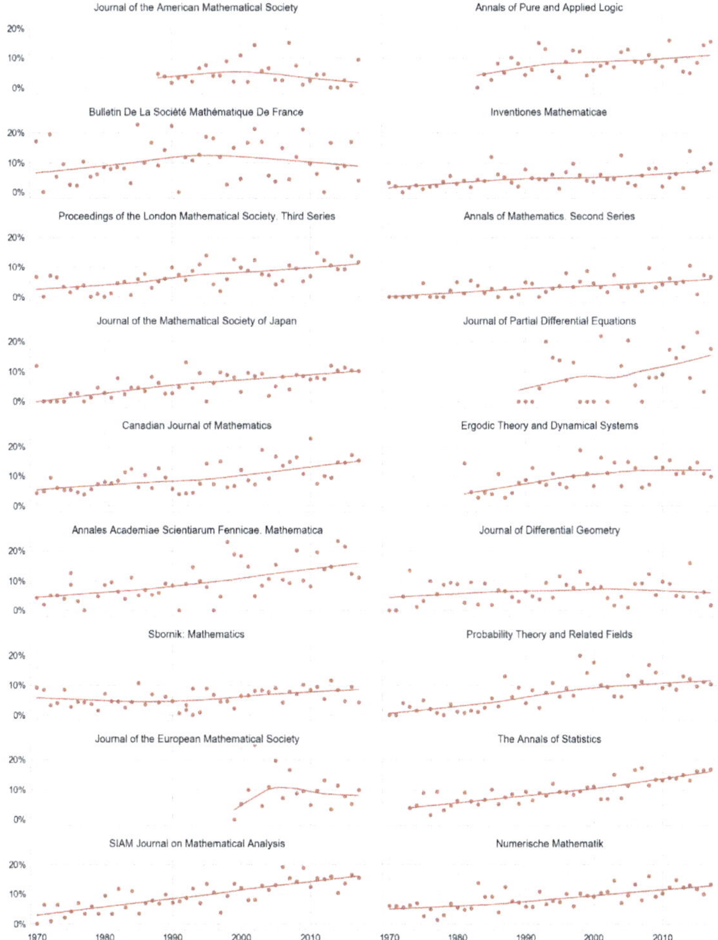

Figure 39: Percentage of fractional authorships from women in top mathematics journal per year since 1970.

Geometry, all journals reveal a (slight) positive trend. The particularly renowned journals Inventiones Mathematicae and Annals of Mathematics, which mainly publish work in pure mathematics, stand out with numbers predominantly in the single-digit range.

To obtain a more comprehensive picture, we have also analyzed the proportion of publications by women in the data set Core Math Priority introduced in 4.1. Recall that this set consists of publications from core math journals currently prioritized by zbMATH's editorial board due to their relevance and high quality. All 18 journals presented in Figure 39 belong to the Core Math Priority dataset. In Figure 40 we see that the proportion of authorships from women has been growing steadily in both the Core Math and the Core Math Priority dataset, which again confirms the trend from Figure 39. However, there remains a gap between the share of women in top journals and their overall presentation as scientific authors in the field.

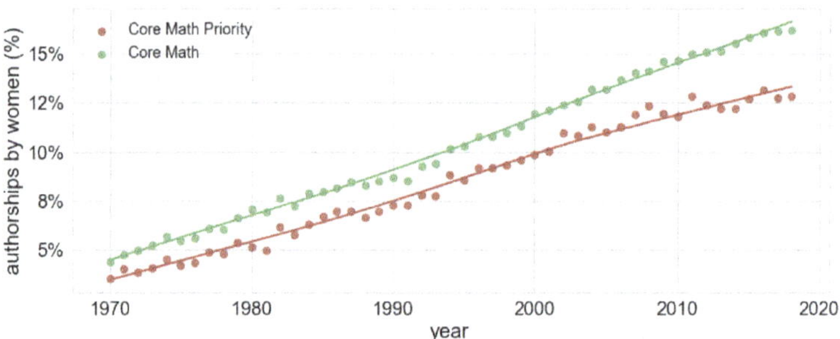

Figure 40: Percentage of fractional authorships from women in the Core Math (green) and the Core Math Priority (red) dataset per year since 1970, fitted using the LOWESS smoothing.

In order to quantify more accurately the evolution over time of the gap shown in Figure 40, we have calculated the relative deviation from the mean per year, i.e. for each year we measure the difference between the proportions of female authorship in both data sets and normalize it by dividing it by the proportion of women in the Core Math baseline set. (For more details on the calculation of the relative deviation from the mean, see Section 4.2.) The relative deviation from the mean is visualized in Figure 41. Starting with a relative deviation of almost -25%, the gap became progressively smaller until the early 2000s, resulting in a relative deviation of -10% to -15%. However, this trend does not seem to be continuing; since 2010, the values have deteriorated and are now in the range of almost -20%.

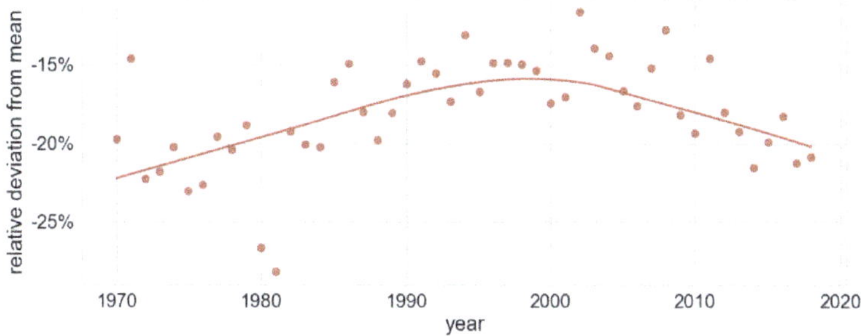

Figure 41: Relative deviation of the annual share of fractional authorships from women in the Core Math Priority dataset from that in Core Math, fitted using LOWESS smoothing.

Astronomy and astrophysics

As explained in Section 5.1 there is no fine-granular classification schemes for publications in astronomy and astrophysics as e.g. the MSC in mathematics. Upon analyzing the journals indexed in ADS (which covers more than astronomy and astrophysics) we have considered all journal titles containing the word "astro" as publications venue belonging to core astronomy. In addition, we have added the journals Nature and Science to this set since they publish high-quality research from various fields, including astronomy and astrophysics. Among these journals, the following six are considered as most relevant for astronomer and astrophysicists community: Monthly Notices of the Royal Astronomical Society, Astronomy and Astrophysics, The Astrophysical Journal, The Astronomical Journal, Nature and Science. This list comprises the five journals covered by [4] and The Astronomical Journal, which participants from our project considered another distinguished publication venue. In contrast to mathematics, these six journals currently cover the majority (70%) of the publications in our core astro set.

Figure 42 displays the percentage of fractional authorships from women in top astronomy and astrophysics journals since 1970. With first author counts the obtained results are

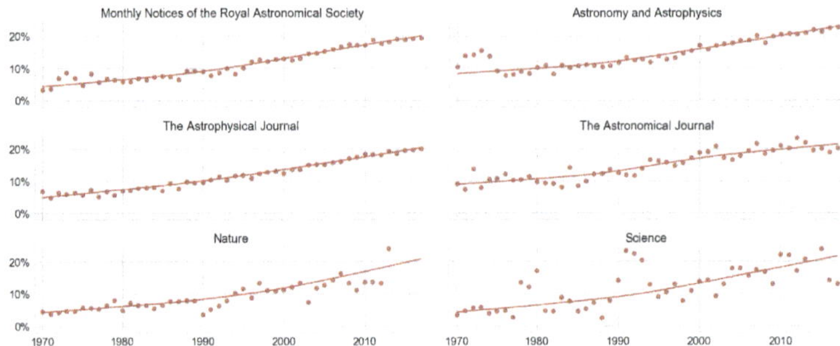

Figure 42: Percentage of fractional authorships from women in top astronomy and astrophysics journals per year since 1970.

very similar, showing slightly fewer female first authors in Science but overall exhibiting the same trends.

In contrast to mathematics and theoretical physics, in astronomy and astrophysics it is apparent that contributions from female researchers have clearly increased over the past decades. All six analyzed journals present women percentages around 20% in recent years, with a continuous increment and comparatively little noise.

Also, compared to the entire set of journals considered core astronomy, the proportion of authorships by women does not deviate from the overall mean in the negative direction anymore. As shown in Figure 43, in the 1970s and 1980s, when these six journals accounted for about 50% of all publications in astronomy and astrophysics, female authorships were still underrepresented. Today, their share in these top journals even slightly exceeds their representation in the entire data set.

Theoretical physics

In theoretical physics, some of the most prestigious journals are the following ten: Physical Review Letters, Physical Review D, Journal of Physics A: Mathematical and Theoretical, Journal of Mathematical Physics, Annals of Physics, Classical and Quantum Gravity, Advances in Theoretical and Mathematical Physics, Reviews of Modern Physics.

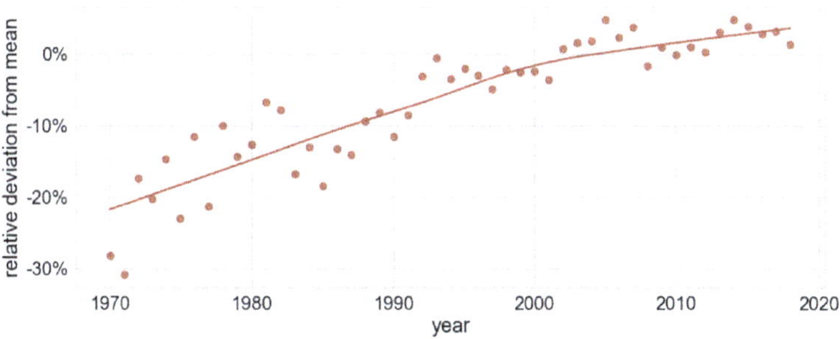

Figure 43: Relative deviation of the annual share of fractional authorships from women in the top six astro journals from that in the entire set of astro journals, fitted using LOWESS smoothing.

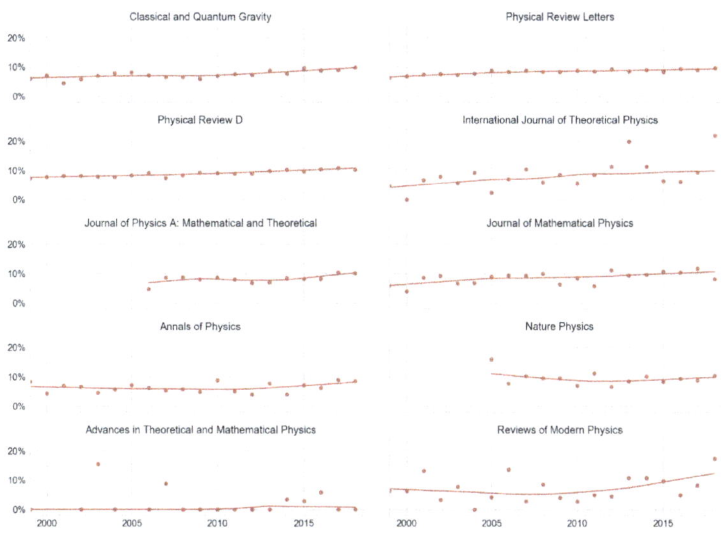

Figure 44: Percentage of fractional authorships from women in top theoretical physics journals per year since 1999.

Figure 44 displays the percentage of fractional authorships from women in top theoretical physics journal over the past 20 years. When using first author counts instead, the obtained results are very similar, showing more noise for first authors in Reviews of Modern Physics but overall exhibiting the same trends.

The situation in theoretical physics appears to be static all throughout the 21st century, with average percentages of women barely reaching 10% and displaying little to no rising tendency. A minor exception is the International Journal of Theoretical Physics, which shows an upward trend but overall rather low figures for women contributions. The situation of female physicists publishing in Advances in Theoretical and Mathematical Physics is rather dismal, with practically no women representation.

It is important to remark that our statistics for theoretical physics are based on the arXiv data, which means that only submissions to the preprint service rather than the final published articles are considered. Although the practice of submitting preprints to the arXiv is rather extended in physics, we can not guarantee that our data basis is comprehensive for all journals displayed above. Nevertheless, we argue that the overall trends and evolution in the discipline can be roughly captured by using the arXiv data as proxy for physics publications.

Chemistry

Some of the top ranked journals in chemistry published either by scientific societies or private publishers are: Chemical Reviews, Nature Chemistry, Journal of the American Chemical Society, Angewandte Chemie International Edition, Chemistry—A European Journal, The Chemical Record. Among experts in the field, these venues have a good reputation that attracts high-quality papers.

Figure 45 (p. 144) displays the percentage of fractional authorships from women in top chemistry journals since 1970. When using first author counts instead, the obtained results are very similar, partially showing more women among first authors, e.g. in the Journal of the American Chemical Society but overall exhibiting the same trends.

The rise of women representation in chemistry over the past five decades is perhaps the most noteworthy among the analyzed STEM disciplines. A clear positive evolution is observed almost consistently in all considered journals, from an initial female percentage below 5% in 1970 up to values in the vicinity of 20% in the 2010 decade. This stark rise is

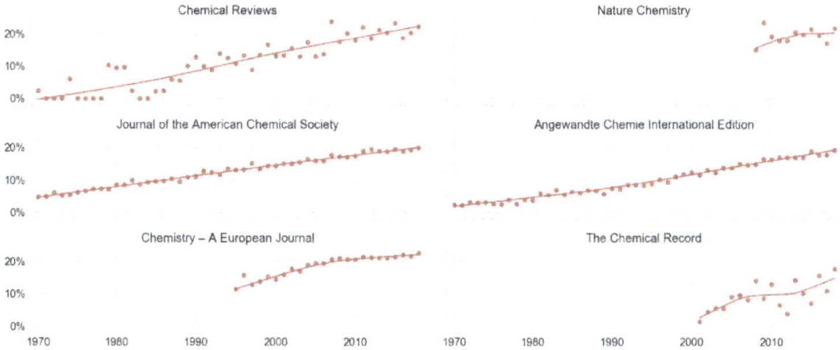

Figure 45: Percentage of fractional authorships from women in top chemistry journals per year since 1970.

nevertheless not trivial to explain. In fact, due to data limitations across the globe, much remains unknown about the status of women chemical scientists on a global level. Several reasons for this are cited in [3], including the lack of an operational definition for chemists and the fact that data collections and repositories in chemistry are disaggregated, disparate, and inconsistent. This makes it difficult to dive deeper into the potential factors for the increased number of female chemists observed in the analysis of the six selected top journals.

Additional resources

Apart from the results shown above, further ad-hoc analyses of journals and gender can be informed by the resources displayed in our visualization website. In `http://gender-publication-gap.f4.htw-berlin.de/journals/collection` it is possible to group selected journals, e.g. the most representative serials in a given discipline, and study how the contributions of women researchers in that collection have evolved over time. We encourage the interested reader to take advantage of this feature to inform their own understanding of publication dynamics in their field.

7.4 Discussion

The comparison of results from the global survey regarding self-reported number of submissions to top journals with the actual publication statistics from selected renowned serials results in a conflicting picture. On one side, while the difference between women and men regarding their perception differs (and the difference is statistically significant), this difference is rather small as shown by the effect sizes computed in 7.2. This means that female and male scientists have the impression that they submit to top journals at comparable rates. In the computed linear model predictors such as the respondent's discipline and country, or the participation in academic activities such as grant committees or editorial boards played a much more important role than their gender. At the same time, the observed percentage of authorships from women in the selected top journals in mathematics and theoretical physics is lower than their overall proportion in the field, as exposed in 7.3. Although the analysis of the survey responses cannot be directly compared to the exploration of bibliographic data for various reasons, we would like to aruge that the responses to the survey cannot explain the (low) amount of women that publish in these renowned journals. The situation, however, is different in astronomy and astrophysics, where the submission practices are quite well aligned with the actual statistics in the selected journals.

There are several arguments for the inconsistency observed in mathematics and theoretical physics: given the fact that participation in the survey was not randomized but rather built on snowball sampling, the survey results are not unbiased and cannot be considered representative of the entire population of scientists who publish academic articles. For instance, it might be plausible that the survey has reached relatively more scientists at institutions with better opportunities for research and cooperation. It is also possible that the self-reported perceptions from men and women regarding their submission practices differ from one another. Additionally, the survey question does not provide a clear definition of what a top journal is, leaving that characterization to the individual perceptions of respondents, which in itself might induce gender-related as well as other types of bias. Nevertheless, the survey represents the perceptions of a large number of scientists and therefore has a certain weight, regardless of the lack of statistical representation. We therefore cannot deduce from the survey that the underrepresentation of female authors in top journals in mathematics or theoretical physics stems from their lower submission rates.

What role potential biases in the process of publishing might play cannot be deduced from the available data. There is a large body of research examining and criticizing the current state of peer review, including discussions of potential biases and possible explanations for the underrepresentation of women as authors. The works [14, 5, 8] provide a good starting point for a deeper study of the topic. The articles [7, 11] further provide valuable insights into the particularities of peer review in mathematics, which is in many aspects presumably quite similar to many areas in theoretical physics. In our opinion, potential existence of biases in the process of publishing in (the selected) top journals in mathematics and theoretical physics can only be effectively clarified through the comparison of submission and acceptance rates broken down by gender. Unfortunately, these are almost impossible to obtain from academic publishers. We thus recommend increasing the transparency of submission and publication processes. The onus is on publishers of research articles to conduct and make available their own investigations on rejection and publication rates in relation to the gender as well as other potentially important features of their submitting authors.

8 Conclusions

The joint data-backed study on publication patterns in STEM was devised with the goals of researching and highlighting commonalities and differences among several fields in the natural sciences. The study was to be based on actual publication data gathered from topical, curated, comprehensive bibliographic repositories, preferably those favoring open publication policies for transparency and reproducibility of results. The ultimate intention of the analysis ought to be aligned with the main questions of the Gender Gap in Science Project. Below we summarize our conclusions regarding important issues for realizing the goals of the project.

Definition and measurement of gender gap

A first fundamental question is how to define a gender gap in science, and which aspects of it can be measured by studying bibliographic metadata. An indisputable fact is that publications matter when making or breaking academic careers and thus have an impact on the observed gender gap in science.

Several metrics regarding academic publications can be assessed and not all of them have the same relevance in different disciplines. For instance, network sizes differ among men and women in mathematics [16] but not so much in astronomy and astrophysics.

Likewise, single author publications play a crucial role for young mathematicians but not so much for astronomers. Yet in some fields it is not the number of coauthors, but the order in the author list that matters and has different implications. This is an example of discipline-specific criteria where field expertise is unavoidable in order to formulate the right questions and arrive at sensible answers. In our analysis we appreciate the fact that we could use the survey's answers, as they are a prime and valuable source of domain-specific knowledge.

We also recognize that our vision suffers from certain Eurocentrism when it comes to defining research questions; for instance we lack local understanding of the common criteria employed for academic promotion in major countries like China or India. Although part of an international project, we were unable to connect with interested individuals who could have shed light on this kind of country-specific details. We recommend such an exchange as a follow-up task, for instance by using a mixed-methods approach combining quantitative approaches with expert interviews.

Due to lack of properly curated and reliable data, there were important aspects of standard publication analysis that we could not investigate. The main one is possibly the study of citation patterns. The primary reason for not including such analysis was the lack of matched citations, without which our only feasible approach would have been that of simply counting them. Furthermore, we agree to a certain extent with the opinion that citation metrics and quality rankings based on them are prone to be misused. Nevertheless, it is true that citations are possibly the most valuable academic currency and certainly play a role in career and promotion processes.

Finally, regarding a definition, there are various aspects to consider when speaking of a gender gap; which ones are appropriate depends on the world region and on the discipline, and sometimes even on the particular community within a discipline. We have provided insights on the gender gap defined by the presence of women in a field by computing proportions of female authorships; we have investigated whether there is a gender gap in the dropout rates that affect typical career lengths of men and women; we have also measured the famous gender productivity gap that examines the amount of research output; and finally we have focused on the gender gap in top journals per discipline. All those aspects are certainly relevant and have been presented in our analyses in a thorough way, for all analyzed disciplines. Moving forward, the analysis of renowned journals and the question about the large observed gender gap among their published authors might become specially relevant, as science policy decision makers in some countries have started to shift the focus away from pure counting and more towards quality of scientific output. More subjective aspects of the gender gap in STEM fields and those not directly measurable via bibliographic metadata, like issues related to missing role models, feelings of critical exclusion, harassment, and low enrollment and retention rates, among others, fall beyond the scope of what our analysis could provide.

We believe that it is crucial to understand the overall dynamics per disciplines and regions, which is why in our analysis we first present many results independent of gender. Without this context it is difficult to adequately interpret the results. For instance, the knowledge that certain countries are mostly absent from renowned journals in a field informs us that looking at the presence of women therein is uninformative with regards to the gender gap in said countries. This is the case of mathematics in Africa, a continent that is essentially excluded from the core mathematics literature. It is only in conjunction with the whole, ungendered picture of a scientific discipline that insights about the particular role of women in it can emerge.

The gender gap in science in geographical zones, in particular in less and more developed countries

Unfortunately, most bibliographic services are still not very well equipped with granular information on authors' countries of work and residence. zbMATH has invested substantial efforts in recent years into gathering more and better affiliation data; nevertheless, the majority of said information is available solely for the last decade and purely on article level, hence we cannot definitely attribute a country to authors from collaborative publications. Luckily, mathematics is a field with a relatively high rate of single-author publications and for those we have looked at the proportion of women and its deviation from the mean per country. For astronomy and astrophysics, the data basis for affiliations provided by ADS was substantial, thus we could perform our geographic analysis on all authorships with available country information. In the arxiv, the coverage is around a mere 10% and the data quality is insufficient, as the affiliations are not exported from the preprint into its metadata. The source files of the full texts contain more information but its extraction could not be realized within the project's scope due to the convoluted parsing needed for it. Hence we restrict our geographical insights to mathematics and astronomy and need to leave physics outside.

Despite discipline-specific disparities between astronomy and mathematics we observe that countries with the highest relative proportions of women are in Europe. The difference between them is mainly seen in Germany and France, countries that as a whole have a significant scientific weight in both disciplines. Yet the share of authorships from women in the two countries is average in mathematics but more prominent in astronomy and astrophysics. Countries in East and South-Eastern Europe are relatively strong in terms of women's presence. Particularly notable are Italy, Turkey, Romania, as well as Balkan countries like Bulgaria, Serbia and Croatia. It would be interesting to compare these figures with the experiences gathered by the national and regional committees of the respective unions.

With respect to other continents, we have only very few countries with a relatively good representation of women: concretely, for the participation from Africa there is either too little data to provide meaningful statistics or women are strongly underrepresented, especially in astronomy and astrophysics. In Iran, India and China women represent a minority in both disciplines, but specially in astronomy. In most Asian countries the presence of women is low. A positive exception in both fields appears to come from Pakistan. The USA enjoys a leading position in the production of scientific research as a whole, and interestingly, the contribution of its female mathematicians and astronomers does not greatly deviate from the average ignoring gender. In South America the most positive situation for women is seen in Argentina.

The gender gap in science in different disciplines

In all three analyzed research fields we observe increasing proportions of women entering science with each passing year. Drop-out rates, which used to be higher for women, are converging on similar values for both genders. The productivity gap regarding the amount of scientific output is getting narrower as well, although recent cohorts show signs of stagnation. In theoretical physics and mathematics, women from the cohorts 1995-2005 publish at a rate of 85-90% of that of their male counterparts after 10 years of an active academic career. In astronomy and astrophysics the figures show an even more equal picture, with female astronomers publishing at a rate of 95% of what men produce. In all three disciplines, however, the numbers are partially skewed due to the fact that 'top performers' that publish extremely many papers are more frequently found among the male population.

Our analysis of women's presence in renowned journals is a good measure of the gender gap in relation to achieving prestigious academic careers (again, this might be a Eurocentric interpretation). Theoretical physics shows the worst development of all disciplines, featuring very low numbers among the authors of papers in top journals plus no visible improvement over the past three decades. The next discipline by ascending percentage of women is mathematics, which displays a positive trend in about half of the 10 considered journals. Regarding its subfields, applied areas exhibit a better situation for women than the pure ones. In both mathematics and physics, the current proportion of women in the analyzed serials is significantly below their overall share, hinting at a potential bias. This could be originated by lower submission rates by women or by a tendentious acceptance process; unfortunately, lack of transparency on the part of academic publishers makes answering this question very difficult. Astronomy shows an overall positive trend regarding presence of women as authors in top journals and the current numbers seem to be representative of the field as a whole. We might thus ascertain that for astronomy the gender gap is the lowest among the compared disciplines. For chemists we observe a strong rising trend in publications from women in top chemistry journals, but we cannot compare with the overall presence of women in the complete discipline due to the already mentioned absence of bibliographic data at a scale.

The remarks above give us an interesting starting point for further analyses and comparisons. There seems to exist a pattern of fewer women in theoretical disciplines and sub-disciplines while a larger presence is found in applied and collaborative fields. Which factor is played by collaboration and to which extent larger academic networks help women careers thrive? It would be excellent to discuss the figures with experts from the respective fields and to formulate hypotheses that could serve as explanations for the observed differences.

9 Acknowledgements

This part of the project was carried out by Prof. Dr. Helena Mihaljević, Dr. Lucía Santamaría, Christian Steinfeldt, Trang Cao and Marco Tullney, a group of data and computer scientists.

We would like to thank the International Science Council, the project partners and all involved individuals who supported us. Furthermore, we would like to thank the operators of the services zbMATH and ADS for the provision of their data as well as their technical and content support during the project. We would also like to thank all the participants of the Conference on Global Approach to the Gender Gap in Mathematical, Computing and Natural Sciences: How to Measure It, How to Reduce It? for beta-testing this website and providing valuable input and feedback.

References

[1] Herman Aguinis, Young Hun Ji, and Harry Joo. "Gender productivity gap among star performers in STEM and other scientific fields." In: *Journal of Applied Psychology* 103.12 (Dec. 2018), pp. 1283–1306. DOI: 10.1037/apl0000331. URL: https://doi.org/10.1037/apl0000331.

[2] Julia Astegiano, Esther Sebastián-González, and Camila de Toledo Castanho. "Unravelling the gender productivity gap in science: a meta-analytical review." In: *Royal Society Open Science* 6.6 (June 2019), p. 181566. DOI: 10.1098/rsos.181566. URL: https://doi.org/10.1098/rsos.181566.

[3] Lisa J. Borello, Robert Lichter, Willie Pearson, and Janet L. Bryant. "International Status of Women in the Chemical Sciences." In: *Advancing Women in Science: An International Perspective*. Ed. by Willie Pearson Jr., Lisa M. Frehill, and Connie L. McNeely. Cham: Springer International Publishing, 2015, pp. 131–171. ISBN: 978-3-319-08629-3. DOI: 10.1007/978-3-319-08629-3_5. URL: https://doi.org/10.1007/978-3-319-08629-3_5.

[4] Neven Caplar, Sandro Tacchella, and Simon Birrer. "Quantitative evaluation of gender bias in astronomical publications from citation counts." In: *Nature Astronomy* 1 (May 2017). Article number: 0141. URL: https://doi.org/10.1038/s41550-017-0141.

[5] Stephen J. Ceci and Wendy M. Williams. "Understanding current causes of women's under-representation in science." In: *Proceedings of the National Academy of Sciences* 108.8 (2011), pp. 3157–3162. ISSN: 0027-8424. DOI: 10.1073/pnas.1014871108. eprint: https://www.pnas.org/content/108/8/3157.full.pdf. URL: https://www.pnas.org/content/108/8/3157.

[6] R.L. Cooke. *The History of Mathematics: A Brief Course*. Wiley, 2011. ISBN: 9781118030240. URL: https://books.google.it/books?id=wOGh7XPowAMC.

[7] Christian Geist, Benedikt Löwe, and Bart Van Kerkhove. "Peer review and knowledge by testimony in mathematics." In: *PhiMSAMP. Philosophy of Mathematics: Sociological aspects and mathematical practice. Including selected papers of the 3rd PhiMSAMP conference 'Is mathematics special?', Vienna, Austria, 2008*. London: College Publications, 2010, pp. 155–178. ISBN: 978-1-904987-95-6/pbk.

[8] Markus Helmer, Manuel Schottdorf, Andreas Neef, and Demian Battaglia. "Research: Gender bias in scholarly peer review." In: *eLife* 6 (Mar. 2017). Ed. by Peter Rodgers, e21718. ISSN: 2050-084X. DOI: 10.7554/eLife.21718. URL: https://doi.org/10.7554/eLife.21718.

[9] Andri Jackson. "From preprints to E-prints: The rise of electronic preprint servers in mathematics." In: *Notices of the American Mathematical Society* 49.1 (2002), pp. 23–32.

[10] Tobias Kiesslich, Silke B. Weineck, and Dorothea Koelblinger. "Reasons for Journal Impact Factor Changes: Influence of Changing Source Items." In: *PLOS ONE* 11 120.4 (2016), e0154199. ISSN: 1932-6203. DOI: 10.1371/journal.pone.0154199.

[11] Steven G. Krantz, Greg Kuperberg, and Alf van der Poorten. "Three views of peer review." English. In: *Notices Am. Math. Soc.* 50.6 (2003), pp. 678–682. ISSN: 0002-9920; 1088-9477/e.

[12] Vincent Lariviere and Cassidy R. Sugimoto. "The Journal Impact Factor: A brief history, critique, and discussion of adverse effects." In: *arXiv e-prints* (Jan. 2018), arXiv:1801.08992. arXiv: 1801.08992 [cs.DL].

[13] Vincent Larivière, Cassidy R. Sugimoto, Benoit Macaluso, et al. "arXiv E-Prints and the Journal of Record: An Analysis of Roles and Relationships." In: *Journal of the American Society for Information Science and Technology* 65 (Jan. 2014), pp. 1157–1169. DOI: 10.1002/asi.23044. arXiv: 1306.3261 [cs.DL].

[14] Carole J. Lee, Cassidy R. Sugimoto, Guo Zhang, and Blaise Cronin. "Bias in peer review." In: *Journal of the American Society for Information Science and Technology* 64.1 (2013), pp. 2–17. DOI: 10.1002/asi.22784. eprint: https://onlinelibrary.wiley.com/doi/pdf/10.1002/asi.22784. URL: https://onlinelibrary.wiley.com/doi/abs/10.1002/asi.22784.

[15] Helena Mihaljević, Marco Tullney, Lucía Santamaría, and Christian Steinfeldt. "Reflections on Gender Analyses of Bibliographic Corpora." In: *Frontiers in Big Data* 2 (2019), p. 29. ISSN: 2624-909X. DOI: 10.3389/fdata.2019.00029. URL: https://www.frontiersin.org/article/10.3389/fdata.2019.00029.

[16] Helena Mihaljević-Brandt, Lucía Santamaría, and Marco Tullney. "The Effect of Gender in the Publication Patterns in Mathematics." In: *PLOS ONE* 11.10 (Oct. 2016), pp. 1–23. DOI: 10.1371/journal.pone.0165367. URL: https://doi.org/10.1371/journal.pone.0165367.

[17] Staša Milojević. "Accuracy of simple, initials-based methods for author name disambiguation." In: *arXiv e-prints*, arXiv:1308.0749 (Aug. 2013), arXiv:1308.0749. arXiv: 1308.0749 [cs.DL].

[18] Imad A. Moosa. *Publish or Perish. Perceived Benefits versus Unintended Consequences.* Edward Elgar Publishing, 2018. ISBN: 978 1 78643 492 0.

[19] Anne Marie Porter and Rachel Ivie. *Women in Physics and Astronomy, 2019.* Tech. rep. Statistical Research Center of the American Institute of Physics, 2019.

[20] Lucía Santamaría and Helena Mihaljević. "Comparison and benchmark of name-to-gender inference services." In: *PeerJ Computer Science* 4 (July 2018), e156. ISSN: 2376-5992. DOI: 10.7717/peerj-cs.156. URL: https://doi.org/10.7717/peerj-cs.156.

Some Initiatives for Reducing the Gender Gap in Science:

a DATABASE of GOOD PRACTICES

Some initiatives for reducing the gender gap in science: a database of good practices

Regina Kelly[1], Merrilyn Goos[2]

1 – University of Limerick, Ireland
2 – Vice-President, International Commission on Mathematical Instruction; Director, EPI*STEM – the National Centre for STEM Education, University of Limerick, Ireland

Introduction

The main aim of Task 3 was to collect a sample of initiatives that address the gender gap in Science and Mathematics and organise these initiatives as a searchable database. Many initiatives have been developed to enhance the participation of girls and women in these fields, but it is not always clear as to which ones "work" and why. In addition, practices that have been proven effective in one context are not always available for consideration or use by others. Thus the rationale for the Task 3 database was to construct a source of such information that could be shared across countries and cultures, and continually expanded. A further aim was to gather and generate evidence of the effectiveness of the identified initiatives. This is a non-trivial task involving significant research into principles that might define "good practice" and "effectiveness".

Parts of this chapter will be proposed for publication as a peer-reviewed article, with an extended list of references.

In general, initiatives established to meet this challenge are broad ranging from intervention programmes in primary, secondary and tertiary education to industry-based interventions targeted at the workplace.

1 Methodology

The methodology for developing the database had three phases: piloting, development and testing (see Figure 1, p. 159).

In the *piloting phase* (elements 1 to 3 of Figure 1), a draft template for organising the database was created and a small number of initiatives ($n = 6$) was sought from members of the Gender Gap project team to begin to populate the template. The SAGA Science, Technology, and Innovation Gender Objectives List (STI GOL), developed by UNESCO [17], was identified as an initial conceptual schema to capture dimensions of "good practice".

In the *development phase* (elements 4 to 7 of Figure 1), further initiatives were sourced using conference networks, online searches, and targeted requests. Countries in specific regions were targeted through searches using the country name and a combination of key words (STEM, science, mathematics, gender, female, women, girls, mentor, role model, workshop). Emails were sent to initiative coordinators, inviting them to share their knowledge of science and mathematics initiatives in their countries. The websites of each of the scientific unions participating in the Gender Gap project were also searched to identify relevant initiatives for inclusion in the database.

Several existing databases (see Table 1, p. 161, for a summary) were reviewed in order to gain insight into features that should be included in the Gender Gap database. The review revealed an inverse relationship between the amount of information included about an initiative and the number of initiatives in a database: there was either a great deal of information about a few initiatives or minimal information about a large number of initiatives. It was therefore decided to include a moderate number of initiatives with key information, categorising their dimensions and with a web link to the initiative itself.

The most crucial aspect of the development phase involved operationalising the dimensions of "good practice" so that the selected initiatives could be fully described in terms of these dimensions. The initiatives were therefore categorised using a set of primary keys that captured not only basic information such as the web link, discipline(s) and target level(s),

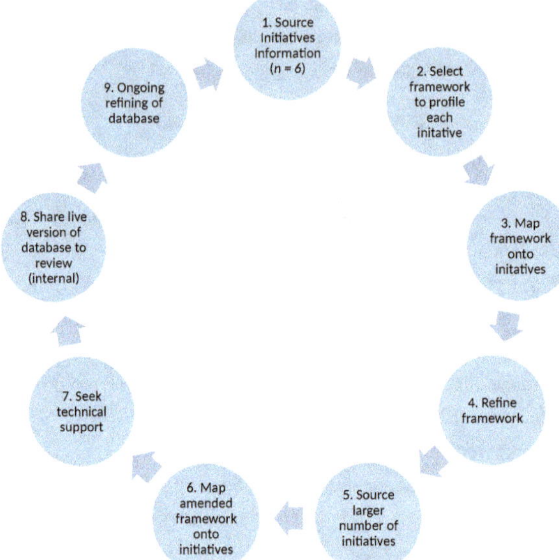

Figure 1: Graphical representation of our methodology.

but also the elements of "good practice" displayed by each initiative as well as evidence of effectiveness (if any). The following primary keys were used:

- Name;
- Acronym;
- Web Link;
- Year Origin;
- Participating Country/s;
- Funding Source;
- Discipline/s;
- Target Level;

- Evidence of Effectiveness and Impact;
- Dimensions of "good practice" (mapped to the Science, Technology and Innovation Gender Objectives List – STI GOL).

One-paragraph (100–200 word) English, French, and Spanish language summaries of each initiative were also prepared and added to the database. Two sample summaries are provided below.

NSF ADVANCE Program

The ADVANCE program seeks to develop systemic approaches to increase the participation and advancement of women in academic STEM careers. The NSF ADVANCE program contributes to the National Science Foundation's goal of a more diverse and capable science and engineering workforce. The NSF ADVANCE program seeks to build on prior NSF ADVANCE work and other research and literature concerning gender, racial, and ethnic equity. The NSF ADVANCE program goal is to broaden the implementation of evidence-based systemic change strategies that promote equity for the STEM faculty in academic workplaces and the academic profession. The NSF ADVANCE program provides grants to enhance the systemic factors that support equity and inclusion and to mitigate the systemic factors that create inequities in the academic profession and workplaces.

#GirlsSTEM

The project #GirlsSTEM was first developed in the Ukraine. The purpose of this project is to encourage girls to not be afraid of choosing a profession in Science and Technology. A community of the top 20 inspirational women in STEM, will share their experiences and knowledge with the girls. 20 Ukrainian women that have gained great success in STEM industry joined the project to inspire and mentor the girls in Ukraine in choosing a STEM education and career. Among them include top managers of technology companies, academics, representatives of ministries, universities and NGOs. As part of the project the inspirational women in STEM will meet 500 senior girls at the age of 13–19 years old in five Ukrainian cities for coaching sessions. During the sessions, the mentors will help girls to develop skills in goal setting and choosing the profession. The main goals are to create role models for young girls and show them that STEM is a place for creativity, and the project will also focus on overcoming gender stereotypes.

In the *testing phase* (elements 8 and 9 of Figure 1, p. 159), a live version of the database was shared with participants at the final conference of the Gender Gap project in Trieste, in November 2019. Two 90 minute sessions were held in one of the ICTP computer laboratories to allow conference participants to explore the pilot version of the Good Practice database, to provide feedback on how to improve it, and to propose additional initiatives that could be added. The suggested improvements were grouped into

1. improving presentation and navigability;

2. improving search functionality; and

Table 1: Sample databases evaluated for design features.

Name	Initiative Type	No. initiatives
Plotina[1]	Good practices for work and personal life integration	25
EIGE[2]	gender mainstreaming strategies	97
Scientix[3]	Science Education Projects	> 650
WorldWideLearn[4]	Initiatives Bringing Women Into STEM	15
Soroptimist[5]	Projects	4
Practising Gender Equality in Science[6]	Gender Equality in Science	109

1: `http://www.plotina.eu/work-life-integration-good-practices/`

2: `https://eige.europa.eu/gender-mainstreaming/good-practices`

3: `http://www.scientix.eu/projects`

4: `https://www.worldwidelearn.com/education-articles/15-innovative-initiatives-bringing-women-into-stem.html`

5: `https://soroptimist-projects.org/portfolio_category/healthandfoodsecurity/`

6: `http://www.pragesdatabase.eu/`

3. adding and verifying entries.

The final version of the database is to be hosted on the IMU/CWM website, and project partners will be able to make a link from their websites to the database.

2 Results

Features of the database at the end of the development phase are described in terms of the regions and countries represented, the spread of disciplines targeted, the dimensions of "good practice" that were defined via modifications to the STI GOL, the distribution of "good practice" Gender Objectives that were addressed, and evidence of effectiveness.

Table 2: Geographical distribution of database initiatives.

Region and countries	No. initiatives
African group *(South Africa, Nigeria, Kenya, Ethiopia, Namibia)*	5
Asia-Pacific group *(Japan, India, China, Philippines, United Arab Emirates)*	7
Eastern European group *(Czech Republic, Poland, Ukraine, Hungary, Bulgaria)*	5
Latin American and Caribbean group *(Brazil, Mexico, Chile, Colombia)*	5
North American group *(United States of America, Canada)*	8
Oceania group *(Australia, New Zealand)*	1
Western European group *(France, Spain, United Kingdom, Germany, Austria Netherlands, Italy, Serbia, Switzerland, Denmark, Ireland, Belgium, Sweden Estonia, Finland, Norway, Portugal, Macedonia)*	21
American *(North America, Mexico)*	1
European *(East, West)*	1
Global	3
Scientific bodies	10
Total initiatives	67

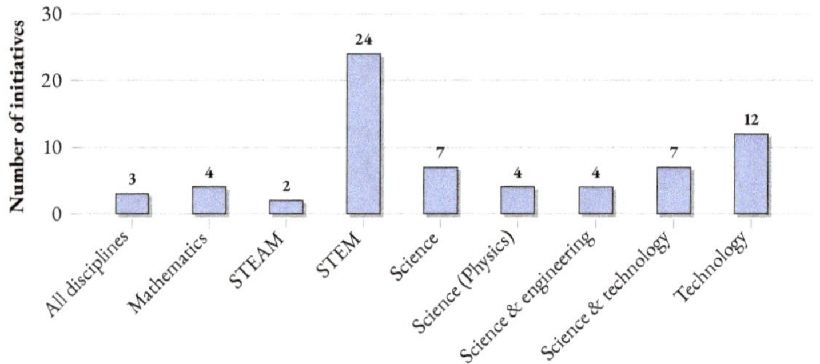

Figure 2: Distribution of disciplines of database initiatives.

2.1 Regions and Countries

At the end of the development phase there were are 67 gender initiatives from more than
44 countries in Africa, the Asia-Pacific, North America, Latin America and the Caribbean,
Oceania, Eastern and Western Europe (see Table 2, p. 162). Initiatives from ten peak
scientific bodies were also included in the database.

2.2 Disciplines

Nearly half the database initiatives claim to target STEM or STEAM, with an additional
three addressing all disciplines and not just science/mathematics. The remaining initiatives
are specific to either science (sometimes specifically physics), mathematics, technology, or
a combination of science/engineering or science/technology (see Figure 2, p. 163).

2.3 Dimensions of "Good Practice"

The SAGA Science, Technology and Innovation Gender Objectives List (STI GOL) published by the United Nations Educational, Scientific and Cultural Organization [17] was
used as an initial conceptual schema to capture dimensions of "good practice" regarding
each initiative. As STI GOL was originally created with the intention of classifying policies
and their associated instruments, some adaptations were made to the four of the seven

objectives and their sub-categories for the purpose of structuring the Gender Gap project database. A summary of the changes that were made to these objectives is presented below. The complete list of modified subcategories for each objective is then provided (with the objectives renames as dimensions of "good practice").

> *Objective 1.* Change perceptions, attitudes, behaviours, social norms and stereotypes towards women in STEM in society.

This objective should also refer to Science, Technology, Engineering and Mathematics stereotypes, rather than just referring to stereotypes towards women in STEM. In respect to gender diversity and STEM, the fundamental issue is that stereotypical views of the type of person who engages with STEM disciplines do not align with how females typically see themselves. It is important to make this distinction as it is possible that STEM stereotypes rather than just gender stereotypes can deter females from STEM. For example, Cheryan et al. found that female role models who embodied STEM stereotypes negatively influenced female participation in STEM [5].

A subcategory was added to acknowledge the influence of families and communities on changing attitudes towards STEM. Families and communities are crucial in the objectives to change perceptions, attitudes, behaviours, social norms and stereotypes towards women in STEM in society as promoting STEM careers to girls might be contrary to cultural expectations and norms. Parents are influencers in students' education and career decisions, and so it is important to target any stereotype they may have about STEM disciplines being more suited to males.

A subcategory was added to acknowledge outreach activities aimed at developing scientific literacy in communities. Research studies have provided evidence that scientific literacy is correlated to interest and engagement in science learning; therefore to change negative perceptions about STEM it is important to encourage public participation in activities that increase scientific literacy.

> *Objective 2.* Engage girls and young women in STEM primary and secondary education, as well as in technical and vocational education and training.

© Léa Cooler

Figure 3: Parents encourage math-learning daughter.

Several subcategories were added under this objective to acknowledge various strategies that engage girls and young women in STEM primary and secondary education.

- *Promote mentoring programmes.* Mentoring is a valuable support to students from underrepresented groups [7, 10, 20] and should therefore be encouraged.

- *Develop females' confidence and skills in leadership, communication, and critical thinking.* Females report they are under-confident in their capabilities compared to their male classmates [8]. Student confidence is an important indicator of science subject choice and success [12]. The development of skills required for STEM professions can also increase females' confidence in their capabilities to engage in a STEM career.

- *Promote equal access to STEM subjects in schools.* While many studies focus on student participation rates, schools can limit or facilitate subject choices [15] or participation in advanced subject levels. For example, schools can gender-type subjects [1] by promoting physics to male students and biology to females.

- *Provide work shadowing opportunities.* Programmes for secondary school students to experience the professional world of STEM present opportunities to redefine gender identities in science and challenge gender and STEM stereotypes that discourage females from pursuing STEM.

- *Promote STEM networks.* Peer groups can act as a means to develop positive values about STEM that endorse females' sense of belonging in STEM fields. Females can feel isolated from STEM groups that are dominated by males.

Objective 3. Promote access to and retention of women in STEM higher education at all levels.

Subcategories were added that expand on the recruitment and retention strategies stated in the original objective. While the additional subcategories are similar to those added to *Objective 2*, as they are situated in the higher education context, they may have different purposes. For example, in higher education mentoring programs may have greater emphasis on career pathways rather than subject choice.

Objective 4. Promote gender equality in career progression for scientists and engineers (S&E).

This Objective was expanded to include STEM academics specifically. The lack of women in senior STEM academic roles has been reported by Athena Swan [18].

Subcategory 4.7 was expanded to acknowledge differential gender-based effects of obstacles experienced by males and females. Obstacles may be experienced by both male and females but are more detrimental to females. For example, short-term contracts for early career researchers affect both male and female research staff. However, a short term contract can have different impacts on males and females based on social norms and values: females may be deterred from these positions due to the lack of benefits such as maternity leave.

Subcategories were added for strategies that promote gender equality in career progression.

- *Mentoring.* The mentoring of STEM professionals is an important means of accelerating employees' careers so that they progress to more senior roles [3, 21].

                                     A database of good practices

- *Gender representation.* It is important to promote gender representation in STEM as male dominated environments can discourage females from joining or remaining in a discipline [2].

- *Gender bias training.* Gender stereotypes are generally consistent in countries [19] with men portrayed through adjectives associated with agency and women described using adjectives associated with communality. Bias training is important as biased workplace practices inhibit women progressing in their career [11]. It is important to educate both men and women as research reports both sexes are prejudiced against females [6, 16].

- *STEM networks and role models.* Sociologists use the term capital to refer to the social advantages gained from being part of a social group [4]. Females in STEM can feel isolated from their male colleagues in instances where they are the minority, having a decreased access to the support of a STEM network [9].

- *Scholarships and awards.* The Matilda Effect, a term first coined by Rossiter [14], describes the disproportionate number of science awards and prizes received by males compared to females. More recent research shows that this bias is still prevalent [13].

- *Industry skillsets.* Deficiencies in personal and interpersonal skills act as barriers to female progression in careers and can be used an indicators about whether a female will remain in STEM. There is a need to provide training to staff to develop these skills to advance in their STEM career.

- *Female networks.* Significant gender differences exist in networking patterns. In some STEM disciplines woman may lack professional networks which can impede their career progression.

Dimensions of "good practice" in addressing the gender gap (modified STI GOL)

Bold text identifies new or modified subcategories, and numbers in parentheses after each subcategory indicate how many of the database initiatives matched this classification.

> *Dimension 1.* Change perceptions, attitudes, behaviours, social norms and stereotypes towards women in STEM in society.

1.1 Promote awareness of and overcome non-conscious and cultural gender biases widely expressed as gender stereotypes, among scientists, educators, policy-makers, research organizations, the media, and the public at large. **Broaden to include raise awareness of equal opportunities (5)**

1.2 Promote visibility of women with STEM qualifications, and in STEM careers, especially in leadership positions in governments, business enterprises, universities, and research organizations **(3)**

1.3 Mainstream gender perspectives in science communication and informal and non-formal STEM education activities, including in science centres and museums **(7)**

1.4 **Promote strategies that engage of families/communities in STEM careers promotion to girls might be contrary to cultural expectations and norms (3)**

1.5 **Promote strategies that engage females in a community to develop scientific literacy and knowledge of social scientific issues (3)**

> *Dimension 2.* Engage girls and young women in STEM primary and secondary education, as well as in technical and vocational education and training.

2.1 Promote S&E vocations to girls and young women, including by stimulating interest, fostering in-depth knowledge about S&E career issues, and presenting role models **(30)**

2.2 Mainstream the gender perspective in educational content (teacher training, curricula, pedagogical methods, and teaching material) **(6)**

2.3 Promote gender-sensitive pedagogical approaches to STEM teaching, including encouraging hands-on training and experiments **(2)**

2.4 Promote gender balance among STEM teachers **(0)**

2.5 Promote gender equality in STEM school-to-work transitions **(0)**

2.6 **Promote mentoring of young girls by higher education or career STEM professionals (11)**

                                          A database of good practices

2.7 **Promote workshops that develop females confidence and other skills (leadership, communication, and critical thinking) (5)**

2.8 **Promote equal access to subject in schools (particularly single sex schools) (0)**

2.9 **Provide work shadowing opportunities in second level (1)**

2.10 **Promote networks of female students (secondary) (3)**

> *Dimension 3.* Promote access to and retention of women in STEM higher education at all levels.

3.1 Promote access of and attract women to STEM higher education **recruitment initiatives (information)** (including Masters and Ph.D.), including through specific scholarships and awards **(12)**

3.2 Prevent gender bias in the student admission and financial aid processes **(0)**

3.3 Promote retention of women in STEM higher education at all levels, including through gender-sensitive mentoring, workshops and networks **(4)**

3.4 Prevent gender-based discrimination and sexual harassment at all levels, including Masters and PhD **(0)**

3.5 Promote gender equality in international mobility of students **(0)**

3.6 Promote day care/child care facilities for students, particularly at STEM higher education institutions **(0)**

3.7 **Promote mentoring of higher education students (7)**

3.8 **Promote strategies that aim to develop female confidence and other skills (leadership, communication, and critical thinking) (0)**

3.9 **Provide training to undergraduates to in outreach and advocacy in promoting STEM education (1)**

3.10 **Provide career information to graduate students (1)**

> *Dimension 4.* Promote gender equality in career progression for scientists and engineers (S&E).

4.1 Ensure gender equality in access to job opportunities, recruitment criteria and processes **(3)**

Figure 4: Equal career progression opportunities?

4.2   Promote equal work conditions through, among others **(4)**

4.3   Ensure gender equality in access to opportunities in the workplace **(2)**

4.4   Promote work–life balance **(1)**

4.5   Promote gender equality in international mobility of post-docs and researchers, and facilitate women's return **(1)**

4.6   Promote gender balance in leadership positions in S&E occupations (including decision making and research) **(3)**

4.7   Promote transformations of STI institutions and organizations (structure, governance, policies, norms and values) aimed at achieving gender equality. **This should be expanded to include obstacles that may be experienced by both male and females but are more detrimental to females, for example short term contracts (lack of benefits maternity leave etc.) (2)**

4.8   Ensure gender equality in S&E professional certifications, in particular in engineering **(0)**

4.9   **Promote mentoring of STEM professionals (5)**

4.10 **Promote gender representation in the sector (4)**

4.11 **Promote gender bias training to STEM professionals (2)**

4.12 **Promote initiatives that increase female STEM networks/role models at professional level (7)**

4.13 **Promote scholarships and awards at professional level (6)**

4.14 **Develop industry skillsets (for example, public speaking) (3)**

4.15 **Promote female networks (2)**

Dimension 5. Promote the gender dimension in research content, practice and agendas.

5.1 Establish specific gender-oriented R&D programmes, including research on gender in STEM and on the gender dimension of the country's research agenda and portfolio **(5)**

5.2 Incorporate gender dimensions into the evaluation of R&D projects **(2)**

5.3 Promote gender-sensitive analysis in research hypotheses and consideration of sex of research subjects **(0)**

5.4 Promote gender responsive and gender-sensitive research dissemination and science communication, including through science centres and museums, science journalism, specific conferences, workshops, and publications **(4)**

Dimension 6. Promote gender equality in STEM-related policy-making.

6.1 Ensure gender balance in STEM-related policy design (decision makers, consultative committees, expert groups, etc.) **(5)**

6.2 Ensure gender mainstreaming and prioritization of gender equality in STEM- related policy design, monitoring and evaluation **(8)**

Dimension 7. Promote gender equality in science and technology-based entrepreneurship and innovation activities.

7.1 Promote gender equality in access to seed capital, angel investors, venture capital, and similar start-up financing **(0)**

7.2 Ensure equal access to public support for innovation for women-owned firms **(0)**

7.3 Ensure visibility of women entrepreneurs as role models **(1)**

7.4 Ensure women's access to mentorship and participation in the design and implementation of gender-sensitive training in entrepreneurship, innovation management, and Intellectual Property Rights **(1)**

7.5   Promote networks of women entrepreneurs and women's participation in entrepreneurship networks **(3)**

7.6   Promote gendered innovation approaches **(0)**

7.7   Promote external incentives and recognition for women-led innovation and acceptance of women innovators in society **(0)**

7.8   Promote gender equality in the access and use of enabling technology, in particular information and communication technology **(1)**

7.9   Promote a gender balanced workforce and equal opportunities in start-up companies **(0)**

2.4 Distribution of "Good Practice" Dimensions

Figure 5 (p. 173) shows the distribution of "good practice" dimensions that characterise the initiatives in the database. It is not surprising to see the lowest numbers of initiatives characterised by dimensions 5–7 since these might be less relevant to the "good practice" interests of the database's intended users (parents, schools and others who influence the careers of girls and women). The specific strategies that were most commonly observed (each has more than ten entries in the database) are:

2.1   Promote vocations to girls and young women in primary and secondary education (30 initiatives);

3.1   Promote access of and attract women to STEM in higher education (12 initiatives);

2.6   Promote mentoring of young girls by higher education or STEM professional (11 initiatives).

2.5 Evidence of Effectiveness

An important aspect of the database is to identify initiatives that represent "good practice". Yet only 10% (15%) of these initiatives have measured the impact of their programme, and only a further 4% (6%) plan to measure impact. For project managers, measuring impact provides information about the overall effectiveness of a programme and insight about further improving its outcomes. Measuring impact provides information to potential participants about the value of a programme. Providing impact evidence demonstrates

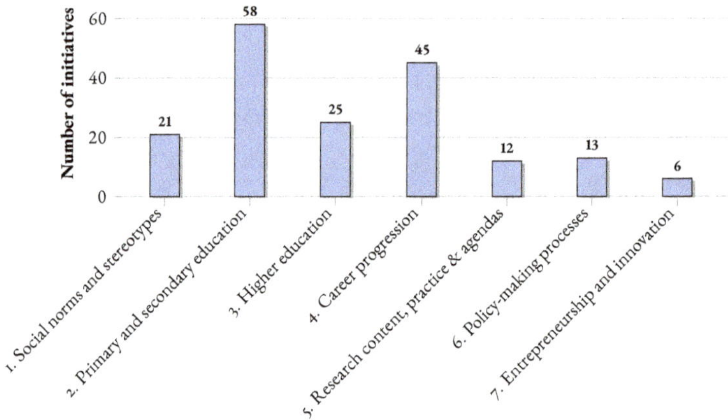

Figure 5: Distribution of "good practice" dimensions in final database.

to stakeholders, policy makers and funding institutions that a particular programme can contribute to positive change regarding the gender gap in Science and Mathematics.

Impact refers to more than just the activities and resources developed by an initiative. Impact is typically evidenced in two ways: (a) outcomes, such as uptake of resources or changes in policy resulting from the initiative; and (b) benefit, such as improvement in social or economic participation and outcomes for females in the STEM disciplines.[1] Examples of initiatives that have provided evidence of impact and how this was measured include the Institute of Physics' evaluation of Project Juno and the WiSci Girls' STEAM Camps.[2]

---

[1] Australian Research Council, *Research impact principles and, framework*, http://www.arc.gov.au/research-impact-principles-and-framework# Definition.

[2] Project Juno, http://www.iop.org/policy/diversity/initiatives/juno/index.html; WiSci Girls' STEAM Camps, https://www.girlup.org/wisci/#sthash.M30s02F3.dpbs.

References

[1] H. Ayalon. "Math as a gatekeeper: Ethnic and gender inequality in course taking of the sciences in Israel." In: *American Journal of Education* 104 (1995), pp. 34–56.

[2] S. Banchefsky and B. Park. "Negative gender ideologies and gender-science stereotypes are more pervasive in male-dominated academic disciplines." In: *Social Sciences* 2.7 (2018), p. 27.

[3] R. A. Berk, J. Berg, R. Mortimer, B. Walton-Moss, and T. P. Yeo. "Measuring the effectiveness of faculty mentoring relationships." In: *Academic Medicine* 80 (2005), pp. 66–71.

[4] P. Bourdieu. "The forms of capital." In: *Cultural theory: An anthology*. Ed. by I. Szeman and T. Kaposy. Oxford, UK: Wiley-Blackwell, 1986, pp. 81–93.

[5] S. Cheryan, J. O. Siy, M. Vichayapai, B. J. Drury, and S. Kim. "Do female and male role models who embody STEM stereotypes hinder women's anticipated success in STEM?" In: *Social Psychological and Personality Science* 6.2 (2011), pp. 656–664.

[6] S. Correll, S. Benard, and I. Paik. "Getting a job: Is there a motherhood penalty?" In: *American Journal of Sociology* 112 (2007), pp. 1297–1338.

[7] D. L. DuBois, B. E. Holloway, J. C. Valentine, and H. Cooper. "Effectiveness of mentoring programs for youth: a meta-analytic review." In: *American Journal of Community Psychology* 2.30 (2002), pp. 157–197.

[8] S. L. Eddy and S. E. Brownell. "Beneath the numbers: A review of gender disparities in undergraduate education across science, technology, engineering, and math disciplines." In: *Physical Review Physics Education Research* 12 (020106 2016).

[9] H. Etzkowitz, C. Kemelgor, and B. Uzzi. *Athena unbound: The advancement of women in science and technology*. Cambridge, UK: Cambridge University Press, 2000.

[10] P. Gurin, E. L. Dey, S. Hurtado, and G. Gurin. "Diversity and higher education: Theory and impact on educational outcomes." In: *Harvard Education Review* 3.72 (2002), pp. 330–366.

[11] M. E. Heilman. "Gender stereotypes and workplace bias." In: *Research in Organizational Behavior* 32 (2012), pp. 113–135.

[12] R. Ivie, R. Czujko, and K. Stowe. "Women physicists speak: The 2001 international study of women in physics." In: *Women in physics: Proceedings of the IUPAP international conference on women in physics*. Ed. by B. K. Artline and D. Li. Melville, NY, USA: American Institute of Physics, 2002.

[13] A. E. Lincoln, S. Pincus, J. B. Koster, and P. S. Leboy. "The Matilda effect in science: Awards and prizes in the US, 1990s and 2000s." In: *Social Studies of Science* 42 (2012), pp. 307–320.

[14] M. W. Rossiter. "The Matthew Matilda effect in science." In: *Social Studies of Science* 23 (1993), pp. 325–341.

[15] E. Smyth and C. Hannan. "School effects and subject choice: The uptake of scientific subjects in Ireland." In: *School Effectiveness and School Improvement* 3.17 (2006), pp. 303–327.

[16] R. E. Steinpreis, K. A. Anders, and D. Ritzke. "The impact of gender on the review of the curricula vitae of job applicants and tenure candidates: A national empirical study." In: *Sex Roles* 7–8.41 (1999), pp. 509–528.

[17] UNESCO. *The SAGA Science, Technology and Innovation Gender Objectives List (STI GOL), SAGA Working paper 1*. Paris, 2016. ISBN: 978-92-3-100154-3. URL: https://unesdoc.unesco.org/ark:/48223/pf0000245006.

[18] Equality Challenge Unit. *Annual Review of 2011*. London, UK, Apr. 2012. URL: https://www.ecu.ac.uk/wp-content/uploads/external/annual-review-2011.pdf.

[19] J. E. Williams and D. L. Best. *Measuring sex stereotypes: A multinational study*. Revised edition. Beverley Hills, CA, USA: Sage Publications, 1990.

[20] Z. S. Wilson, L. Holmes, M. R. Sylvain, et al. "Hierarchical mentoring: A transformative strategy for improving diversity and retention in undergraduate STEM disciplines." In: *Journal of Science Education and Technology* 1.21 (2012), pp. 148–156.

[21] J. W. Yen, K. Quinn, C. Carrigan, E. Litzler, and E. A. Riskin. "The ADVANCE mentoring-for-leadership lunch series for women faculty in STEM at the University of Washington." In: *Journal of Women and Minorities in Science and Engineering* 13 (2007), pp. 191–206.

Impacts of the Gender Gap in Science Project in AFRICA, ASIA and LATIN AMERICA

Silvina Ponce Dawson

Igle Gledhill

Mei-Hung Chiu

© Léa Castor

Impact of the Gender Gap in Science project in Africa, Asia and Latin America

Silvina Ponce Dawson[1], Igle Gledhill[2], Mei-Hung Chiu[3]

1 – Departamento de Fisica, FCEN-UBA & IFIBA, CONICET-UBA
2 – University of the Witwatersrand, Johannesburg, South Africa
3 – National Taiwan Normal University Graduate Institute of Science Education

Introduction

The vision of the International Science Council is that science is a global public good. In this regard it has among its aims to promote

> *"the continued and equal advancement of scientific rigour, creativity and relevance in all parts of the world".* [3]

The ISC is fully committed to help achieve the 17 ambitious goals of the 2030 Agenda for Sustainable Development of the United Nations that aim, among other things, to reduce inequality and poverty. ISC strongly believes that, to advance in this regard,

> *"scientific knowledge from across all disciplines must have a major role [...] identifying transformative pathways towards the sustainable and equitable use of planetary resources".*[1]

Gender equality is one of the 17 goals of the 2030 agenda. As stated by the UN, it

> *"is not only a fundamental human right, but a necessary foundation for a peaceful, prosperous and sustainable world".*[2]

---

[1] The ISC at the UN High Level Political Forum 2019, `https://council.science/current/news/the-isc-at-the-un-high-level-political-forum-2019/`.

[2] United Nations, *"Sustainable Development Goal 5: Achieve Gender Equality and Empower All Women and Girls,* `https://www.un.org/sustainabledevelopment/gender-equality/`.

Sharing this vision, the Global Gender Gap in Science Project has worked towards exchanging knowledge and resources across the developing world, especially in the three regions where the ISC has regional offices: Africa, Asia and Latin America. In particular, one of the first activities of the project was the organization of workshops in these three regions to incorporate a local perspective into its three tasks.

In this chapter we describe the impact that these workshops and the project as a whole has had so far in these continents.

1 Africa

The Africa regional workshop of the Gender Gap project took place at the African Institute of Mathematical Sciences, AIMS, Muizenberg, Cape Town, South Africa, on 1–2 December 2017. The organizers were Igle Gledhill, Marie-Françoise Roy, Marie-Françoise Ouedraogo, Rachel Ivie, Danielle Gondard-Cozette and Rene January.

The Gender Gap project organizers would like to record their gratitude to AIMS, the ICSU (now International Science Council) Regional Office for Africa (ROA) and the ICSU Board of South Africa. AIMS contributed free venues (plenary and five breakaway), all meals for 20 people, most airport transfers, accommodation bookings, and organizational support. ICSU-ROA hosted a welcoming Meet-and-Greet event on the evening of 30 November, at which the Director, Dr Daniel Nyanganyura, was able to welcome those participants who had already arrived. The Vice-Chair of the ICSU Board of South Africa, Dr. Rudzani Nemutudi, opened the Workshop and stayed to participate. Dr. Simukai Utete welcomed the participants, on behalf of the Director of AIMS SA, Dr. Barry Green.

The aims of the workshop were to use our collaboration to

1. check the survey questionnaire to make certain that it addressed the main issues in the African region correctly,

2. provide routes for dissemination of information about the survey in the countries and regions, and

3. collect lists of existing good practices suitable for our region, and our countries.

Figure 1: Participants of the African regional workshop, December 2017.

Participants attended from Algeria, Burkina Faso, Botswana, Cameroon, Ethiopia, France, Kenya, Lesotho, Morocco, Madagascar, Malawi, Nigeria, South Africa, Swaziland, Uganda, United States, and Zimbabwe. In total, 39 participants attended. Of these, 5 were men and 34 were women. These partners were represented: IMU, IUPAP, IUPAC, IAU, IUBS, ICIAM, UNESCO and the SAGA project, OWSD, GenderInSite (by a video presentation), and ACM. In addition, SAWISE (South African Women in Science and Engineering) and WISWB (Women in Science Without Borders) were represented.

The project, the three tasks, and the survey were introduced. The workshop was unusual in that more than half of the time was spent at work in breakaway sessions. There were six consecutive breakaway sessions including five on the survey and one on task 3 (Database of good practices). The groups were small – about 7 people – and worked very well together on specific tasks, giving short report backs, with details provided on paper and in presentations.

Figure 2: Countries represented at the African regional workshop (left) and one of the breakaway sessions of the African regional workshop (right).

As Survey leader, Rachel Ivie led the Joint Global Survey working groups. Danielle Gondard-Cozette, introduced task 3, which is in early stages. Of the 11 partners, 8 made very short presentations on their Union or organization and its involvement in the project. The participants were, in many cases, very senior scientists, and the quality of the interaction was very high. During this African workshop, participants worked to ensure that the questions on career disruptions included the realities that scientists throughout Africa face. Breakaway groups recorded detailed comments and short presentations. Once completed, results from each of the sessions were organized and compared to determine the final survey instrument. In all cases, contributions from all attendees and insights from different disciplines and countries were shared, further helping to refine the global survey to be culturally appropriate both in terms of language as well as in substance. As a result, responses were expanded to include health, conflict, natural disasters, and other continent-specific answers, and Arabic was added as a language.

A few of the participants were invited to interact with AIMS women students at a mentoring lunch. Evaluation forms were distributed to all the participants, and 23 were returned. Of these 20 replied that they agreed or strongly agreed that they learned about the Gender Gap project. In terms of the first aim, 22 participants were very positive that they had been able to contribute to the draft questionnaire. The feedback was judged to be of a high quality and useful for future planning.

Figure 3: Snapshots of the African regional workshop.

2 Asia

This section is partly based on the article entitled *Gender Gap in Science* by M.-H. Chiu, M.-F. Roy, & H. Liaw that appeared on Chemical International [2].

The Gender Gap in Mathematics and Natural Science Project Regional Workshop took place on November 6–7, 2017 at the National Taiwan Normal University in Taipei, Taiwan.

There was a total of 38 participants, coming from different backgrounds in mathematics and science of twelve countries (namely, Australia, China, France, India, Israel, Japan, Korea, Malaysia, Nepal, Taiwan, Thailand, and USA). The participants included representatives from the supporting organizations as well as local scholars and local science teachers. The main purpose of this workshop was to inform participants about the project, to get input from the regional scientists, to ensure integration of the insights and regional priorities into the project, to adjust the survey to local realities, to organize the dissemination of information about the project, to establish contact with individuals interested in project participation, and organize the dissemination of project information.

To achieve the goals stated aforementioned, an overall project overview was delivered by Prof. Marie-Françoise Roy from IMU and Prof. Mei-Hung Chiu from IUPAC as the representations of lead Unions 1 and 2. Prof. Marie-Françoise Roy further introduced discussion of public communication and social media for the project. Dr. Rachel Ivie of American Institute of Physics (AIP), who is responsible for the design of the global questionnaire, held several sessions in the two-day workshop to ensure attendees' understanding of the purposes and functions of the questionnaire as well as to address their concerns and suggestions for the survey. IUPAP had conducted a similar study previously, and so Dr. Ivie presented a talk on the history of the survey, highlighting past results, presenting the goals of the new survey, and providing an overview of its methodology. She also presented

Figure 4: Group photo of the Asia-Pacific regional workshop at NTNU, November 2017.

previous survey distribution efforts and outlined best practices for distribution. Following these presentations, she helped the participants to understand the reach of the audience for the new survey and to discuss required languages for the survey instrument. During her session, Dr. Ivie also held group activities during which participants provided more detailed and specific inputs to the questionnaire after reaching group based consensus. The activities were greatly successful with ample useful inputs from all groups.

From IMU, Prof. Nalini Joshi (Australia) presented *Reflections on Gender Diversity in Mathematics*; Prof. Neela Nataraj (India) provided *Gender Gap in Natural Sciences and Mathematics – Challenges and Initiatives?*; and Prof. Dhana Thapa (Nepal) presented *Mathematics and Nepalese Women: A Glimpse*.

From IUPAC, Prof. Chiu (Taiwan) introduced the structure and missions of IUPAC as well as the women in chemistry awards by IUPAC. Prof. Rachel Mamlok-Naaman (Israel)

Figure 5: Lectures during the Asia-Pacific regional workshop.

gave an introduction to IUPAC and also an overview of women's participation in sciences in Israel. Meanwhile, Dr. Supriya Saha (India) presented some *Best Practices for Promoting Female Scientists in India*.

Hailing from ICIAM, Prof. Amy Novick-Cohen (Israel) overviewed *Gender Gap in Applied Math, Math and Materials, in Israel and Abroad*. Dr. Kazue Sako (Japan) informed us on the JSIAM activities that were designed to encourage women researchers; and Prof. Guiying Yan (China) gave us a glimpse into the state of Chinese female scientific research.

For IUPAP, Prof. Youngah Park (Korea) provided some ideas on *How to Promote Gendered Innovations in Global S&T Landscapes*. Prof. Prajval Shastri (India) discussed *The Gender Gap in Science: Do the Causes Lie Within?*; and Prof. Ling-An Wu (China) gave an introduction on *Lecture Tours by Women Physicists in China*.

In addition, Prof. Saeko Hayashi (IAU; Japan) talked about the *Mighty Minority of Women in Astronomy in Japan*. Drs. Parawee Lekprasert and Chalita Thanyakoop (SAGA; Thailand) described *STEM and Gender Equality in Thailand*. Prof. Tien Huynh (IUBS; Australia) gave a personal account of *My journey in STEMM*. Prof. Amita Chatterjee (IHUPST; India) presented *Gender Gap in Mathematics and Science: Some Observations from the Indian Perspective*. And Prof. Catherine Lang (ACM; Australia) introduced ACM-W regarding its highlights, objectives, and activities.

Among the local scholars, Prof. Chia-Li Wu (Taiwan) gave a presentation on the surveys of gender gap in Asia, and Prof. I-Ling Chang (Taiwan) described gender gap in science and engineering schools in Taiwan.

Figure 6: Small group discussion during workshop (clockwise from bottom left: Prof. Guiying Yan [ICIAM; China], Prof. Catherine Lang [ACM; Australia], Prof. Chia-Li Wu [Local Scholar; Taiwan], Dr. Hsiao-Lan Chung [Local Teacher; Taiwan], and Prof. Prajval Shastri [IUPAP; India].

A questionnaire after the workshop was conducted. The results of overall feedback from attendees proved positive. One attendee stated:

"The workshop was excellent, informative, well-structured and very well-organized."

Other attendees described the workshop as *"warm and constructive"*, *"a very effective and productive workshop"*, and having given him/her

"a new perspective of other disciplines in science".

It seemed that the missions to inform participants about the project, to get input from the regional scientists, to establish contact with individuals interested in project participation, and to build regional networks were accomplished. The accomplishment was seen in the final number of respondents to the survey.

Other quantitative measures also revealed an overwhelmingly positive feedback among our attendees, with most attendees confirming that they felt the program of the workshop to be well-organized (Average 4.88/5). Respondents of the post-workshop survey strongly felt that they have learned from the workshop gender gap research across various countries (Average 4.8/5) and issues across different disciplines (Average 4.56/5). Through this workshop, respondents stated that they have shared their ideas for the future work for the project (Average 4.44/5), and believed that they have made contribution to the draft questionnaire (Average 4.56/5) and the results of the questionnaire will bring concrete recommendation for policies (Average 4.56/5). By bringing so many attendees from across Asia and Australasia, respondents also believed that they have made new connections with participants through the workshop (Average 4.72/5).

The Taipei workshop was the first of the workshops and had provided valuable and essential inputs from scientists/mathematicians of Asia and Australasia. With additional inputs from scholars and science practitioners from Africa and South America, the questionnaire would not only be more representative but also address cultural nuances and regional concerns, making the finalized questionnaire a truly global instrument.

So far, the project reinforced evidence that the global gender gap still exists. Preliminary results of the survey for chemistry and mathematics showed that women report lower salaries, more career interruptions, and more instances of discrimination [1]. A symposium on *Does Gender Gap in STEM⁺ Education still Exist? – A Global Gender Gap Project* was organized by N. Tarasova (IUPAC Past-President) and Mei-Hung Chiu (IUPAC member of Executive Committee) for the IUPAC World Congress, Paris, 7–12 July, 2019. Three speakers (Gillian Butcher, Nathalia Fomproix, & Mei-Hung Chiu) from IUPAP, IUBS, and IUPAC respectively, were invited to report preliminary results of the survey at the IUPAC World Congress.

Finally, thanks to the ISC, supporting organizations, National Taiwan Normal University, and the Chemical Society Located in Taipei provided financial support for the Taipei workshop. Also, thanks to all the participants for providing the insightful inputs to the project.

3 Latin America

The Latin American Workshop of the Gender Gap in Science Project took place in Bogotá, Colombia, on November 22–24, 2017.[3] Immediately before, there was another workshop on Professional Skills for Young People in Science and Engineering at the same premise.[4] This gave the opportunity for both workshops' participants to share an activity in the morning of November 22nd. On that occasion the Gender Gap in Science Project was presented to a broader public. The presentation was followed by a discussion on feminism in Latin America and how those ideas could help advance the agenda of the project. The Latin American Workshop of the Gender Gap in Science Project was attended by 30 people from 9 Latin American countries and one from the USA. All of the scientific unions that were part of the project at the time and the then ICSU Regional Office for Latin America and the Caribbean were represented at the Workshop. Participants worked on the survey questionnaire, discussed options for the analysis of patterns of publications and made presentations of initiatives of their unions, scientific societies or national institutions aimed at helping reduce the gender gap in STEM, improve the workplace environment and increase inclusiveness. A discussion in smaller groups was organized around the following issues: organization of networks and workshops, charters, protocols to handle cases of gender violence, implicit bias and the popularization of science with a gender perspective. All the participants were very enthusiastic and felt that the work should not end with the workshop. For this reason, it was decided to keep in touch through social media, to write a book with information on good practice initiatives within Latin America, to collect and share this information on a website,[5] that had been set up for the meeting and to organize a new workshop once the results of the Global Survey of Scientists were available.

Based on the active discussions held in Bogotá, we first updated the material available on the site.[6] We then created the Facebook group *Gender Gap in Science Latin America* which currently has 166 members and through which information on publications and activities is shared. Right now, the website contains detailed information on the Bogotá Workshop

---

[3]Latin American Workshop of the Gender Gap in Science Project,
`https://emcyt_icsu017.uniandes.edu.co/index.php/evento-especial-icsu`.
[4]Workshop on Professional Skills for Young People in Science and Engineering,
`https://emcyt_icsu017.uniandes.edu.co/index.php`.
[5]Gender Gap in Science project Latin America, `http://wp.df.uba.ar/ggapsla/`.
[6]Gender Gap in Science project Latin America, `http://wp.df.uba.ar/ggapsla/`.

Figure 7: Participants of the Latin American regional workshop, Bogotá, November 2017.

including files of some of the presentations of the meeting, a list of good practice initiatives undertaken in Latin America and the rest of the world and a description of the various activities related to the project that have been carried out in Latin America.

One of the main activities that came out of the Bogotá workshop was the edition of a book [4] with contributions by the participants and other representatives of scientific unions in the region. Thirty authors from Argentina, Brazil, Colombia, Costa Rica, México, Perú and countries outside the region contributed to the book which was edited by Lilia Meza Montes of Puebla, México and Silvina Ponce Dawson of Buenos Aires, Argentina and was published by the Mexican Physical Society (ISBN 978-607-98384-3-0) with funds provided by the global project. The book is entitled *The Gender Gap in Mathematics, Computing and Natural Sciences. An Approach from Latin America*. It has an introduction by the coordinators of the Global Project, a prologue by the organizer of the Bogotá Workshop and 14 chapters describing strategies that have been implemented in the region to reduce the gender gap in STEM at various levels: within scientific societies and unions, within countries, within regional networks, etc. At the end, there are several photographs of the activities that are described in the book and testimonies by participants of these activities. A preliminary version of the book was presented in Lima during the Workshop on Professional Skills for Young Scientists that was held in this city in October, 2018. The final version of the book was presented in São Paulo, Brazil in October 2019 and

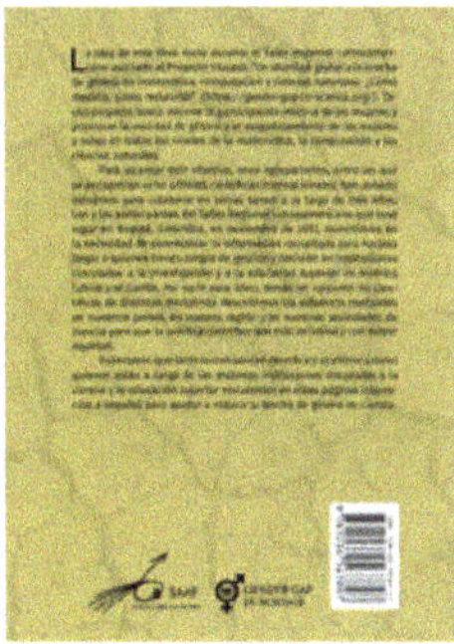

Figure 8: Cover of the book containing contributions of the various participants of the Latin American regional workshop.

is downloadable from the website mentioned before. Two hundred and fifty copies of the book have been printed out to be distributed in academic institutions of Latin America and within the contributors of the chapters. It is expected that the contents of the book will be useful for academic and scientific institutions, societies and the scientific community at large to introduce the necessary changes to help reduce the gender gap and increase diversity in STEM.

The other important activity that came out of Bogotá was the decision to organize a new workshop in 2019, once the first results of the Global Survey would be available. To this end, a proposal was presented to the International Centre for Theoretical Physics South American Institute for Fundamental Research, ICTP-SAIFR, of São Paulo, Brazil by the end of 2017. The proposal was approved and two workshops in a row, similarly to what had happened in Bogotá, took place at this prestigious institution on October 7–11, 2019: a Workshop on Professional Skills for Young Scientists (Oct 7–9) and a Workshop on Increasing Diversity in STEM (Oct 9–11). The number of applicants exceeded all expectations and not all of them could be accepted because of lack of space. Talks by consolidated scientists, interactive activities and discussion sessions took place during the first of these two workshops. The results of the Global Survey for Latin America, a description of the analysis of patterns of publications and the way the database on good practices is tagging the initiatives that have been collected so far were presented during the

Figure 9: Participants of the workshop on professional skills for young scientists and Alice Abreu of GenderInSite giving the weekly colloquium of the IFT, São Paulo, Brazil, October, 2019

Figure 10: Round table on ethnicity and Laura Merner from the AIP Statistical Research Center describing the results of the Global Survey for Latin America, São Paulo, Brazil, October, 2019.

second one. There were poster and oral contributions by participants and a round table on ethnicity. Taking advantage of our activity, the weekly colloquium of the Institute of Theoretical Physics (IFT) that is located within the same premises as the ICTP-SAIFR was given by one of our invited speakers, Alice Abreu from GenderInSite. This gave workshop participants and organizers the opportunity to share the issues that they were discussing with the larger community of the institution that was host of the workshops.

As with previous workshops, the workshops were characterized by a great emotional openness intermixed with valuable discussions on how to increase diversity in STEM. The use of social networks was emphasized, especially by the youngest participants, and a

Figure 11: Activities during the conference on the project that took place at the ICTP in Trieste, Italy, November, 2019. From left to right: Silvina Ponce Dawson and Alicia Dickenstein in front of the poster on activities in Latin America to help reduce the gender gap in STEM; a selfie by Lilia Meza and the presentation of the Latin American book during the discussion session on the Americas.

hashtag and the Facebook group, Increasing Diversity in STEM, were created to exchange information and stay in touch. There are plans to have a new Workshop on Professional Skills for Young Scientists in Chile in 2020.

Various Latin American women in STEM participated in the *Conference on Global Approach to the Gender Gap in Mathematical, Computing and Natural Sciences: How to Measure It, How to Reduce It?* that took place in Trieste, Italy, in November, 2019. Many of them presented posters on the situation of women scientists in their countries or on activities they took part in to help reduce the gender gap in STEM. There was also a poster on the region as a whole describing several of the activities that have been taking place in Latin America to make the practice of STEM more inclusive and diverse.

During the conference there was also a session on the Americas that was attended by participants from Argentina, Brazil, Chile, Colombia, Mexico and Peru. After discussing differences and similarities between the responses to the Global Survey by people from North, Central and South America and analyzing briefly the results on the analysis of publication patterns segregated by gender, people shared their knowledge on best practice initiatives across the Americas. Given the very good connections that already existed among the participants from Latin America and the Caribbean, the discussion focused on possibilities of collaboration across the whole continent. In this regard, the participants agreed that it would be good to look into the possibility of having an Athena Swan-like[7] program covering the Caribbean and North, Central and South America. They also

---

[7] Athena Swan, `https://www.ecu.ac.uk/equality-charters/athena-swan/`.

decided to look into various funding possibilities (through the USA National Science Foundation or the American Association for the Advancement of Science, for example) to start new collaborations or expand existing ones within all the Americas. In summary, the final conference of the project also provided a platform to start new interactions to advance towards a more equitable practice of STEM in Latin America.

4 Conclusions

In summary, the Global Project on the Gender Gap in STEM had a very large impact in Africa, Asia and Latin America, potentiating activities that were already taking place in these regions and initiating new ones.

References

[1] Mei-Hung Chiu, Marie-Françoise Roy, Irvy M.A. Gledhill, and Rachel Ivie. "Are we all ready to get rid of gender inequality?" In: *L'Actualité Chimique* 422 (2019), pp. 25–27.

[2] Mei-Hung Chiu, Marie-Françoise Roy, and Hongming Liaw. "The Gender Gap in science." In: *Chemistry International* 40.3 (2018), pp. 14–17. DOI: 10.1515/ci-2018-0306.

[3] International Science Council. *Advancing Science as a Global Public Good. Action Plan 2019–2021*. Paris, France: International Science Council, 2019. URL: https://council.science/wp-content/uploads/2019/12/Advancing-Science-as-a-Global-Public-Good_ISC-Action-Plan-landscape.pdf.

[4] Lilia Meza Montes and Silvina Ponce Dawson, eds. *La brecha de género en Matemática, Computación y Ciencias Naturales: Un abordaje desde América Latina*. México: Sociedad Mexicana de Física, 2019. ISBN: 978-607-98384-3-0.

Report of the Final Conference
of the Gender Gap in Science Project,
on 4-8 November 2019 at ICTP

Marie-Françoise Roy

Colette Guillopé

© Léa Cash

Report of the final conference of the Gender Gap in Science project

Colette Guillopé[1], Marie-Françoise Roy[2]

1 – French Association Women & Science, Honor President
2 – Chair of the International Mathematical Union Committee for Women in Mathematics

Aim of the Conference

The first aim of the final conference was to report on the methodology, tools produced and results of the project, and formulate recommendations and open questions based on its results. All the people giving talks were informed of the results of the survey, data analysis of publications, and compilation of good practices. The talks were not expected to be speculative about what the gender gap is, but to refer to the results gathered and produced within the project. A second aim of this conference was to make it possible for attendees to learn how to use our tools and answer their own questions.

1 Participation

There were 102 participants, 90 female and 12 male. This was a huge success, since the project approved by ICTP was anticipating 74 participants.

The total number of applicants was 353, with 45 males. The fact that the final proportion of males was slightly smaller than their proportion among applicants comes from the priority given to geographical diversity, so that most of the time only one participant per country was selected.

From a geographical point of view, there were 26 participants from Africa, 15 from Asia, 36 from Europe, 11 from Latin-America, 11 from North America and 3 from Oceania. A total of 57 countries were represented. Unfortunately there were no participants from Japan, while the number of responses from Japan to our global survey of scientists was significant.

From a thematic point of view, there were 40 representatives from IMU, 19 from IUPAP, 9 from ACM, 6 each from IUPAC and IAU, 4 from OWSD, 3 from IUBS, 2 each from ICIAM and GenderInSite, 1 each from IUHPST, UNESCO, SISSA and ICTP and 7 others.

The larger number of participants from Mathematics and Physics comes from the fact that both IMU and IUPAP have efficient networks for women in their disciplines and a specific committee for women. The members of the corresponding networks were well known to the organizers of the meeting and were natural candidates to represent their countries.

Financial support for the meeting came from the budget of the Gender Gap project through IMU, from the ICTP and SISSA. Some unions and partners of the Gender Gap project contributed directly to the budget by paying for the participation of their members.

2 Program

The program of the meeting was mainly concentrated on reporting on the results of the project but included also some invited talks. Various interactive sessions in little groups were organized: computer sessions, discussions by discipline or geographical zones, sessions for mini-projects using the tools of the project and a World Cafe. A colloquium talk was part of the program as well as a movie, a roundtable at SISSA, and a social dinner downtown.

3 Welcome and distribution of preliminary report

Participants were welcomed by the new ICTP director Atish Dabholkar, and Marie-Françoise Roy, one of the directors of the conference. The preliminary report of the project was distributed, and the importance of discussing and improving the recommendations of the project was highlighted.

Marie-Françoise Roy also informed the participants of a diplomatic issue, saying:

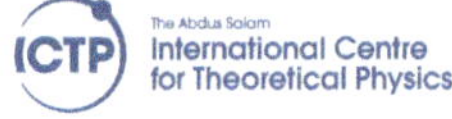

Figure 1: Conference participats.

"According to UN and UNESCO instructions, one conference director Mei-Hung Chiu was not allowed by ICTP to attend the meeting. The reason is that she has a non-UN passport, being from Taiwan. Fortunately the regulations are not the same at SISSA and you will meet her in person during our roundtable. Her welcome video is on the Gender Gap in Science website `https://gender-gap-in-science.org/`*."*

4 Presentation of the results of the project

The results of the tasks of the project were presented by Rachel Ivie and Susan White for the Global Survey of Scientists [12], Helena Mihaljević for the Joint data-backed study on publication patterns [16] and Merrilyn Goos for the Database of Good Practices [11]. There were presentations by Silvina Ponce Dawson, Marie Françoise Ouedraogo and Lucía Santamaría on the findings of the project with respect to the gender gap in geographical zones [20], less and more developed countries [19], and disciplines [22], also based on the reports of the three tasks included in previous chapters.

The contents of all their talks were extracted from the chapters of the report and can be found there. The main results and open problems also appear in Chapter (pp. 11–36) of this report, and we do not repeat the information here.

5 Colloquium, film, invited lectures and roundtable

5.1 Colloquium talk

Prof. Petra Rudolf, Zernike Institute for Advanced Materials, University of Groningen, presented a fascinating colloquium talk on Molecular Motors and Switches at Surfaces in the framework of ICTP colloquia [21]. The talk was very successful, with about 25 attendees from ICTP on top of the participants from the Gender Gap in Science Project conference. Many questions were asked and a discussion between Petra Rudolf and the students or young researchers from physics at ICTP followed. The following two excerpts are taken from the talk announcement.[1]

Summary of Petra Rudolf's talk

> *Nano-engines and molecular motors form the basis of nearly every important biological process. In contrast to this solution chosen by Nature for achieving complex tasks, all of mankind's present day technologies function exclusively through their static or equilibrium properties. One can therefore easily anticipate that the controlled movement of molecules or parts of molecules offers unprecedented technological possibilities for the future. In this presentation I shall illustrate*

---

[1]ICTP Colloquium on Molecular Motors and Switches at Surfaces,
`http://indico.ictp.it/event/8985/`.

how introducing new concepts, like incorporating a ratchet mechanism, allows for the creation of molecular engines that transcend simple switches. I shall discuss how to build molecular engines that allow movements at the molecular level to be coupled to the macroscopic world, e.g., to transport macroscopic objects like drops of liquid over a surface. Another example are molecular systems that can be triggered to form spontaneously functional structures with a well-defined position on surfaces. I shall discuss molecular switches, which can be addressed with light and charge transfer and show that such systems can be employed for "read and write" functions.

Bibliographical sketch of Petra Rudolf

Petra Rudolf was born in Munich, Germany. She studied Physics at the La Sapienza, University of Rome, where she specialized in Solid State Physics. In 1987 she joined the National Surface Science laboratory TASCINFM in Trieste for the following five years, interrupted by two extended periods in 1989 and 1990/1991 at Bell Labs in the USA, where she started to work on the newly discovered fullerenes. In 1993 she moved to the University of Namur, Belgium, where she received her PhD in 1995 and then quickly moved from postdoctoral researcher to lecturer and senior lecturer before taking up the Chair in Experimental Solid State Physics at the University in Groningen in 2003. Her principal research interests lie in the areas of condensed matter physics and surface science, particularly molecular motors, 2D solids, organic thin films and inorganic-organic hybrids. She has published 239 peer-reviewed articles and 26 book chapters. Dr. Rudolf is the President of the European Physical Society; she was the President of the Belgian Physical Society in 2000/2001 and was elected member of the German Academy of Science and Engineering, honorary member of the Italian Physical Society, Fellow of the Institute of Physics, "Lid van verdienst" (Merit Member) of the Dutch Physical Society and Fellow of the American Physical Society. For her work on molecular motors she received the 2007 Descartes Prize of the European Commission. In 2013 she was appointed Officer of the Order of Orange Nassau by H. M. Queen Beatrix of the Netherlands.

The conversation with Petra Rudolf was continued during the conference, and she was invited to talk for a few minutes about her various activities related to women in science and for reducing the gender gap.

In particular, she gave the following relevant information: the EU Erasmus+-supported Strategic Partnership *Diversity in the Cultures of Physics* has developed a curriculum for summer schools for young female physicists, including a series of teaching modules on Gender & Physics, and a flyer with recommendations on how to make outreach activities more gender inclusive. These products are open access and can be freely used and shared (see attachments). In detail they comprise:

- *Lesson Plans*. Reflections on Gender & Physics: A collection of teaching material on Gender and Physics, which can be used as single lectures or as a series.

- *Diversity in the Cultures of Physics*. A European Summer School Curriculum: Description of the curriculum for an international summer school for young female physicists. Such a summer school serves to support participants in reaching their career goals. Next to individual encouragement there also are the structural conditions for the gender gap in the field and the participants experience possibilities for bringing about change.

- *Making physics outreach more gender inclusive*. A flyer with recommendations on how to make outreach activities gender-inclusive. This flyer is intended for staff who design and carry out outreach activities.

Details about the project can be found here:
```
https://www.physik.fu-berlin.de/diversity-in-physics.
```

5.2 Film: Hidden Figures

The film is a 2016 American biographical drama directed by Theodore Melfi and written by Melfi and Allison Schroeder [15]. It is loosely based on the non-fiction book of the same name by Margot Lee Shetterly about black female mathematicians who worked at the National Aeronautics and Space Administration (NASA) during the Space Race. The film stars Taraji P. Henson as Katherine Johnson, a mathematician who calculated flight trajectories for Project Mercury and other missions. The film also features Octavia Spencer as NASA supervisor and mathematician Dorothy Vaughan and Janelle Monáe as NASA engineer Mary Jackson, with Kevin Costner, Kirsten Dunst, Jim Parsons, Glen Powell, and Mahershala Ali in supporting roles.

5.3 Invited lectures

Anathea Brooks presented a talk about *Recent Developments at UNESCO on Gender Equality* [5]. In summary, the talk contained:

1. an overview of the 2019 revision to UNESCO's Gender Equality Action Plan including UNESCO's standing under the United Nations System-wide Action Plan for Mainstreaming Gender Equality and the Empowerment of Women (GEEW);

2. major projects and activities aimed at promoting GEEW undertaken by UNESCO in all its domains – education, the natural sciences (the main focus), the social and human sciences, culture, and communication and information – in line with the upcoming report, UNESCO and the Promise of Gender Equality; and

3. an update on the STEM and Gender Advancement (SAGA) project which ended in late 2018.

Erika Coppola then explained the ICTP programs and Gender Equality activities at ICTP [8], and Tonya Blowers, the OWSD programs [2].

In her talk *"No longer alone!": Career Development Workshops for Women in Physics* Shobhana Narasimhan presented a very lively report on this interesting and creative ICTP activity, which takes place at ICTP every other year [17].

The participation to these workshops is very often a life-changing experience for the participants.

Tracy Kay Camp reported in her talk *Changing the faces of computing* on her successful initiatives for increasing the number of women in computer science at her home institution, the Colorado School of Mines [6].

In her talk *Present and future: how individuals, policies, institutions, and culture shape the evolving gender gap in science*, Guadalupe Lozano considered examples of how current

<u>Importance of Involving Social Scientists</u>

Anuradha Srinivasan
Cross-cultural learning

World Café format discussions

Maitri Gopalakrishna
Drama therapy

Drama workshops

Figure 2: Importance of involving social scientists (slide taken from Shobana Narasimhan's presentation).

realities and behaviors at the micro- (individuals) and macro-levels (institutions, culture) may affect (or not) the eventual attainment of global gender equity in science [14]. Illustrations included stigmas, beliefs, and other factors impacting use of parental leave policies, and the seemingly inverted gender gap in the service dimension of academic professorships in the United States.

Catherine Jami's lecture on *Some aspects of research by social scientists on the gender gap in science* was particularly important, since interaction with social sciences was an objective of our project, and not much progress had been made in this direction. Her talk covered a variety of topics, including the famous DAST [13].

Quoting her conclusion slide:

"What Are You Taking Away From the Workshop?"

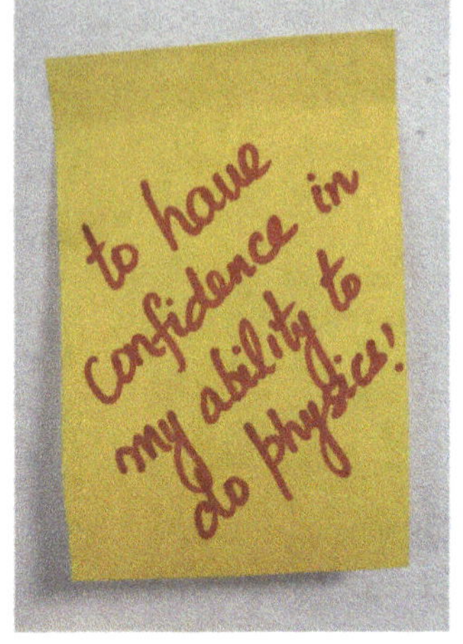

Figure 3: "What are you taking away?" (slide taken from Shobana Narasimhan's presentation).

- *"The past is a foreign country; they do things differently there."*
  (L. P. Hartley, *The Go-Between*)

- Scientific progress does not in itself guarantee the raising of the level of gender awareness.

- The social sciences have developed tools that are very effective for highlighting gender biases and gender gaps.

- Let us all use them!

5.4 Roundtable at SISSA

A roundtable on the gender gap in science in Europe and in North America took place at SISSA. Many members of SISSA attended as well as the participants of the Gender Gap

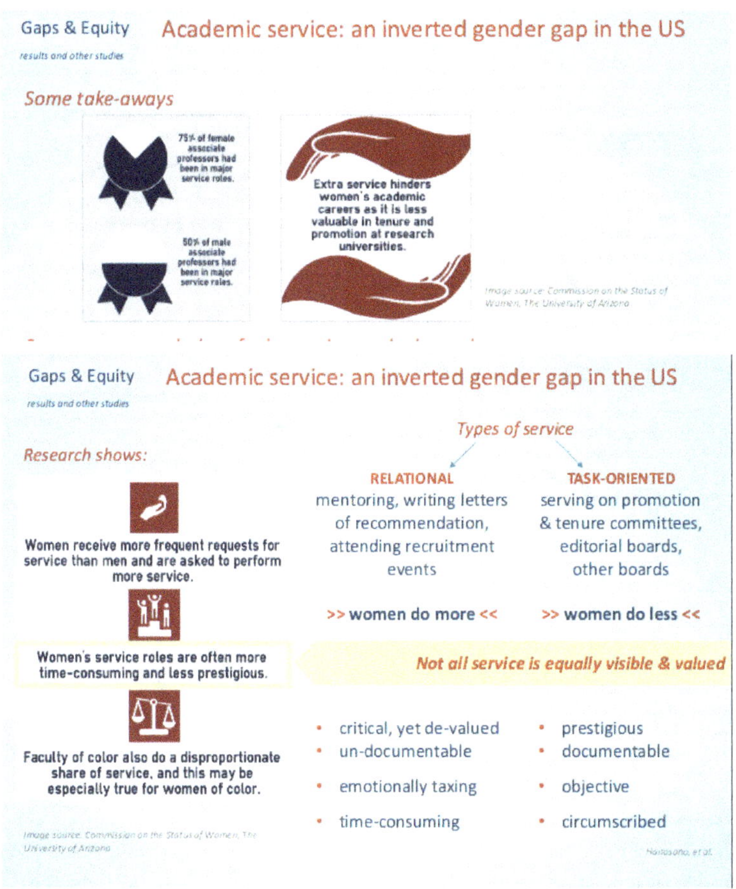

Figure 4: Academic service: an inverted gender gap in the US (slides taken from Guadalupe Lozano's presentation).

in Science conference. The session was chaired by Mei-Hung Chiu. After a short update

The DAST

- The Draw a Scientist Test
- Studies conducted since 1957
- By 1999, "the perception of scientists being male Caucasians working indoors with chemistry [was] still prevalent".

From Chambers, D.W. (1983). "Stereotypic Images of the Scientist: The Draw a Scientist Test". Science Education. 67 (2): 255–265. doi:10.1002/sce. 3730670213

Kevin D. Finson, "Drawing a Scientist: What We Do and Do Not Know After Fifty Years of Drawings," *School Science and Mathematics* 102,7 (2002):335-345 https://doi.org/10.1111/j. 1949-8594.2002.tb18217.x

Figure 5: The *Draw a Scientist* test (slide taken from Catherine Jami's presentation).

by Marie-Françoise Roy on the project, directed at SISSA members, the four panelists launched the discussion.

Silvana Badaloni's presentation focussed on the situation in Italy [1]. The typical and well known scissors diagram in academic institutions, where we see an initial higher proportion of women, dropping systematically along career progression, and resulting in an inverse situation for top hierarchical levels is not valid in STEM since from the start the proportion of women is much smaller than the proportion of men and remains so all along (see the diagram with the proportions of women and men in STEM at the University of Padova, Italy; and the diagram with the proportions of women and men in STEM in EU-28 from *She Figures 2018* [10] in Figure 6, p. 208).

Jean-Pierre Bourguignon, the president of the European Research Council (ERC), reported on the successful initiatives of the ERC to ensure gender balance in their grant

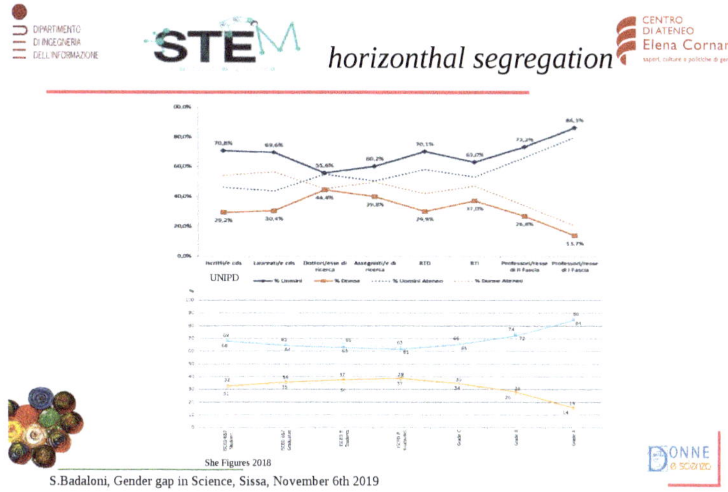

Figure 6: Top: Proportions of women and men in STEM at the University of Padova, Italy; Bottom: Proportion (%) of men and women in a typical academic career in scienece and engineering, students and acacdemic staff, EU-28, 2013–2016 (slide taken from Silvana Badaloni's presentation).

programs [4]. Figure 7 (p. 209) present the proportions of women at the second stage for Starting Grants for years 2015 to 2019.

One key initiative, decided in 2010, was to add 18 months per child to all age-limits for people having taken care of children, which in practice applies mainly to women giving birth, regardless of maternity leave taken (before or after PhD). Indeed, rights to maternity leaves differ a lot from country to country, even within Europe.

Kathryn Clancy, a professor of anthropology who served on the recent National Academy of Sciences Committee to Address Sexual Harassment in the Sciences, presented the report *Sexual Harassment of Women* [18], and summarized its main findings as follows:

- sexual harassment is about gender, not sex;

- the US legal system is inadequate to address this problem;

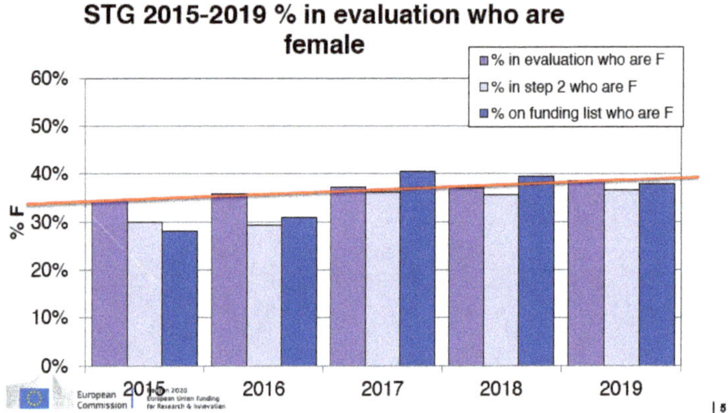

Figure 7: Starting Grant program (slide taken from Jean-Pierre Bourguignon's presentation).

- leadership and culture change are needed.

The diagram in Figure 8 (p. 210) taken from her presentation [7] is striking.

Jodi Tims, the chair of ACM-W, the Association for Computing Machinery's Community of Support for Women in Computing, presented the situation for computer science in USA, which remains atypical compared to other scientific disciplines (see diagram) and the work done by ACM-W chapters in the various parts of the world [24].

6 Contributions of the participants

6.1 Discussions of participants in parallel sessions

Two moments with parallel sessions were organized, by discipline and by continent.

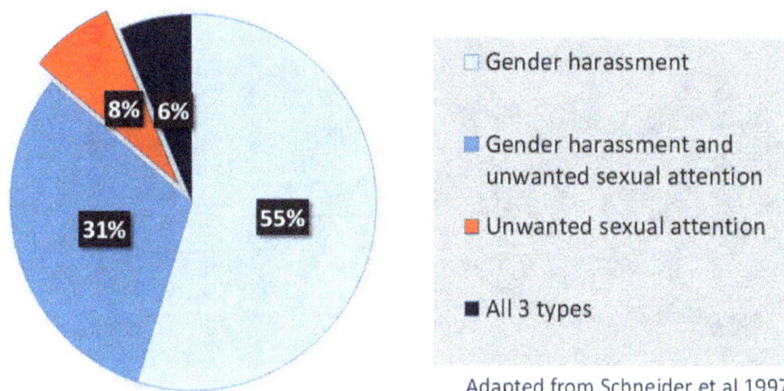

Figure 8: 92% of sexual harassment involves "put-downs" (slide taken from Kathryn Clancy's presentation).

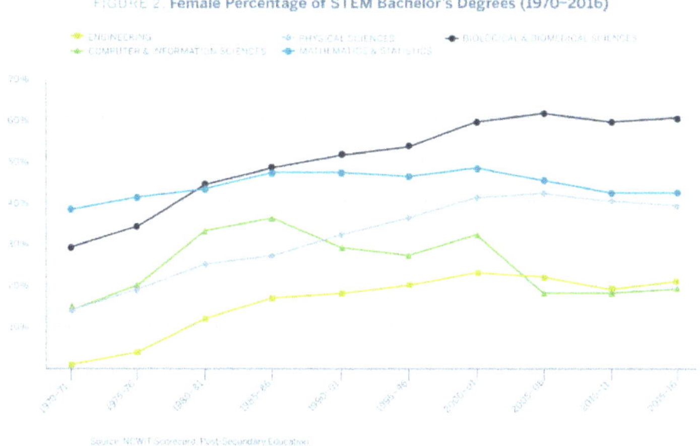

Figure 9: Representation of Women in STEM – US (slide taken from Jodi Tims' presentation).

Figure 10: Group picture of the meeting for Asia and Oceania.

The discussions for disciplines were led by Marie-Francoise Roy (Institut de Recherche Mathématiques de Rennes, IMU) for Mathematics, Gillian Butcher (University of Leicester, IUPAP) and Silvina Ponce Dawson (Instituto de Física de Buenos Aires, IUPAP) for Physics, Francesca Primas (European Southern Observatory, Germany, IAU) for Astronomy, Jodi Tims (Northeastern University, ACM) for Computer Science. Mark Cesa (INEOS Nitriles Process Technology, retired, IUPAC) and Nathalie Fomproix (IUBS) led the discussion on Biology, Chemistry, History of Science. Claudio Arezzo, head of the ICTP Mathematics Group, joined the Mathematics session and presented information on the situation of women in mathematics inside ICTP.

For continents, discussions were led by Igle Gledhill (IUPAP) and Marie Françoise Ouedraogo (African Women in Mathematics Association) for Africa, by Catherine Lang (School of Education, La Trobe University, Australia, ACM) for Asia and Oceania, by Mark Cesa (INEOS Nitriles Process Technology, retired, IUPAC) and Silvina Ponce Dawson (Instituto de Física de Buenos Aires, IUPAP) for America and by Colette Guillopé (LAMA, Université Paris-Est Créteil, France) for Europe.

See reports on these parallel sessions on `http://indico.ictp.it/event/8731/`.

Biographies

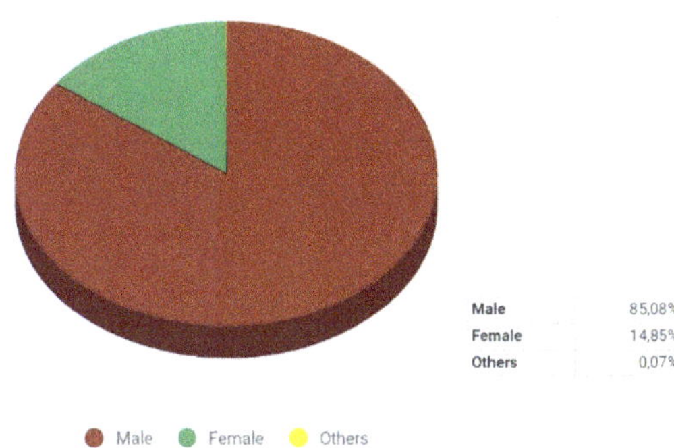

Figure 11: Biographies (slide taken from Camelia Boban's presentation).

6.2 Computer Session

The Computer Session on the Joint data-backed study on publication patterns had the goal to introduce the conference participants to the website that has been developed as part of the project and that visualizes various analyses regarding the publication practices of women and men in different scientific disciplines. The website, currently available at `http://gender-publication-gap.f4.htw-berlin.de`, was explored by the participants, who provided valuable questions and feedback for those involved in creating the website. The task leaders and developers were able to provide explanations and thus to help disseminate the website in the respective communities. The session lasted for two hours and was of great use for the further improvement of the visualizations and the website structure.

6.3 Wikipedia pages for women in science

Camelia Boban, from WikiDonne, Italy, presented in her short talk the Gender Gap in Wikipedia, which is huge, and not only in science [3].

She also presented the many initiatives such as campaigns, meetings, launched to reduce the gap.

She then led a half a day session for about 25 volunteers among the participants entitled *Wikipedia pages for women in Sciences*. The goal of the session was to complete the mostly empty Wikipedia pages of 13 preselected woman scientists (physicists, recommended by the IUPAP). More generally, the session aimed to familiarize the participants (mostly women) with Wikipedia content creating and editing. Most participants had never partaken in such activities and some were even unfamiliar with computers. The first step was, therefore, to set up everyone to their monitors, have them create their own Wikipedia account, and activate some useful tools helpful in the upcoming tasks. The second step was to divide the attendants in 13 groups, each of them working on a given woman scientist. Some people expressed their wish to do slightly different tasks, such as writing the page of someone else, translating or modifying an already existing page, which they did. Finally, some participants became *de facto* helpers for everyone else, thus effectively working on several pages simultaneously. At the end of the session, the group did not manage to finish the pages of all 13 selected scientists, although all their pages have been started. They will be completed and possibly integrated into Wikipedia after further cooperation between their original contributors (the writing participants) and Camelia Boban.

6.4 Exploring the Data base of Good Practices

Merrilyn Goos led two 90-minute sessions in one of the ICTP computer laboratories to allow conference participants to explore the pilot version of the Good Practice database, to provide feedback on how to improve it, and to propose additional initiatives that could be added. A pilot version of the database was available at:

`https://www.mathunion.org/cwm/gender-gap-in-science-database`.

To explore the database, participants were invited to:

1. Browse all initiatives on the database home page;

2. Try the search functions (search by discipline, country, region, target audience);

3. Offer written feedback on how to improve the organisation and functionality of the database (e.g., suggest additional search criteria);

4. Go to the web form and submit information about additional gender initiatives.

Suggestions for improving the database were grouped into three categories:

1. Improving presentation and navigability;

2. Improving search functionality;

3. Adding and verifying entries.

They are going to be implemented to improve the Database.

As a whole the two sessions were very useful, both for people working in the corresponding project and for the participants.

6.5 Poster session

About 30 posters were presented. Their aim was not to present individual research results of the participants but for unions and organizations partners of the project to highlight their activities related to women in science or for participants to describe the initiatives of their national or regional organization for reducing the gender gap. Posters were beautiful and actively discussed.

7 World Cafe discussions

There were about 100 participants distributed into 12 small discussion groups. Each group discussed three questions in successive 30-minute sessions at three tables, each table being facilitated by a table leader. Each participant had received the preliminary report. The aim of the World Cafe was to provide relevant suggestions, coming from the experience of the participants, to supplement the recommendations in the preliminary report by a list of propositions coming from the ICTP conference participants.

Question 1. What are the initiatives you recommend in the direction of instructors and parents?

- Provide parents with early awareness, especially opportunities to learn about science fields they may have thought were unsuitable for their girls.

Figure 12: Poster session.

- Reach parents with material on gender equity and the success of women in STEM. Use toys to build the ability to explore.

- In the home environment teach girls how to negotiate, how to take on team work, and how not to shy away from responsibilities. Teach boys about gender equity.

- Parents often make efforts to protect girls, but should develop girls' self-confidence to defend them from insecurity. Don't push a path based on the objectives (or the failure) of the parent.

- Teach children to handle intimidation in online social networks sites and how to counter boys' overestimation of their abilities, and girls' underestimation, when these occur.

Figure 13: Impressions from the World Cafe discussions (i).

- Teachers and parents should not avoid STEM as a career suggestion for girls, or direct most girls towards health-psychology-education.

- Revise career information, present opportunities for getting a science education, and provide information on the jobs that women in science occupy.

- At schools, include gender issues in curricula, provide gender short courses, workshops, summer schools or picnics for teachers and parents, and create public scientific spaces.

- Make available books and media written by women, biographies of women, and media releases. Avoid books that reinforce the gender gap.

- Educators should receive gender awareness training, and use inclusive language.

- Teachers should track who they are calling on in class to ensure that every student has a chance to participate and that girls speak in class, and should encourage girls in class.

- Develop career counselling and information on opportunities.

- Consider the benefits of single-sex classes.

Question 2. What are the initiatives you recommend in the direction of your local institution?

- The Global Survey has shown that there is a significant problem of harassment and gender-based violence for scientists. Safe laboratories for after-hours work are very much needed. Put in place an ombudsperson, someone to whom complaints can be made, and who acts on them, and is a woman. Protect schoolgirls and university women from violence without compromising their education: find better solutions to stop violence and protect girls and women than closing libraries, labs and campuses to them. Consider campus security for women.

- Address gender equity and equality in relevant institutional policies, with clear anti-harassment policies and lines of action.

- Make public case studies with different regulatory frameworks and cultural contexts.

- Implement effectively and monitor carefully: gender-related data has to be reliable to get the real situation.

- Diversity action plans should have financial consequences if not met.

- Provide grants that are predicated on certification like that of Athena Swan.

- Help women write proposals better to get grants and therefore power.

- To change salary gender gaps, change the way that evaluations and promotions are made. Make selection processes transparent, and ensure female and male representatives are on recruitment committees but provide unconscious bias training for all members. Use quotas if necessary. Make the gender lens the responsibility of a dedicated person on each committee.

- Put in place committees for women in every organization, including countries where culturally women are expected to be married and fit into specific roles. Involve men in identifying barriers and addressing them.

- Assign Gender Champions who have the seniority to make significant change.

- Foster informal and formal networks. Involve both retired scientists, and young voices. Increase gender gap literacy within the different cultures in the organization: there are unlikely to be universal recommendations.

- Make ways for distance PhDs or switching universities for Master's graduate women who are left to stagnate by harassment and discouragement. Retain and promote women onto the staff to reduce harassment in PhD supervision.

- Replace assessment of publications by "bean counting" (i.e. mere counting of all the papers of an individual) by nomination of her or his best 5 papers.

- Make statistics on salaries, loadings, bonuses, hiring and promotion transparent. Monitor support, wellbeing, mentoring and progress of female academics. Provide re-entry grants, resource women returning to their country after a PhD abroad, a research-only year after maternity leave, parental leave, and a child-friendly working environment. Allocate teaching loads with suitable hours for parents.

- It was noted that there is a reverse gender gap in some aspects of academia in some countries.

Question 3. What are the initiatives you recommend in the direction of the national (or beyond) organizations to which you belong?

- Make scientific Unions, members and societies aware of this Gender Gap project and continue to foster action in the coming years.

- Make information available: write ethical manifestos[1] or charters for gender equity and equality; share best practices, and develop toolkits for activities. Train scientific Union staff in gender and implicit bias. Share policy, toolkits and learning to enable member organisations and members (e.g. creating welcoming work environments, how to be a good mentor, guidance for parents and families, etc.).

Figure 14: Impressions from the World Cafe discussions (ii).

- Develop anti-harassment protocols and support services to deal with sexual and gender harassment. Share these since smaller organisations may not have the resources to develop their own.

- In leadership, appoint Gender Champions in the highest positions and in decision-making bodies.

- A committee or chapter for women and/or gender should exist in every organisation, with a certain level of independence, and an assigned budget line. Provide grants, prizes and fellowships specifically for women; mandate representation on award committees; make a quota for the pool of nomination for awards, under which no award will be made; or consider two awards, at least one of which goes to a woman.

- Make policies on funding conferences with representative speaker and panel lists, Scientific Organizing Committees and Local Organizing Committees. Have a reporting mechanism for concerns at the conference. Assign a Gender Champion to monitor these. Develop guidelines for the provision of child friendly arrangements in academic conferences including the provision of childcare facilities, grants for paying for childcare arrangements, family friendly schedules, child friendly social activities, etc. Always hold a women's networking event that is open to all.

- In all outreach programs, make an aim of reducing the gender gap. Provide training in critical thinking. Offer membership to high school girls with outreach to parents.

- Mount campaigns to increase awareness of the benefits to society of reducing the gender gap. When role models are introduced, include diverse backgrounds, ages and those who did not necessarily have a straightforward traditional career, including scientists not working in academia.

- For organizations with publications, adopt humane practices for review that address gender pronouns in addressing the author and reviewer. Use double blind review. Manage constructive feedback on submitted papers.

- Gather information from members: hear disenfranchised groups, and aid in developing plans. Consult with members on policies. Connect members to each other: foster networks and mentorship schemes. Define discontinuous careers better and understand how to translate that to hiring and funding policies.

- This question also elicited responses for government advice and influence, including: use unions to advocate good gender policy; create laws on affirmative action and flexible working, with consequences for those who do not respect them; improve pay for science teachers; change curricula and material; require specialist committees that will systematically check laws, practices and policies for equality and diversity; mandate and resource more school time (compatible with children's educational interests) in places where the common practice is for school to last only half a day; and mandate family leave (maternity, paternity, family care).

- Invite relevant government ministers, secretaries, etc., to gender events for the profession. In order to do this, connect across organisations and scientific Unions.

8 Discussions on the future of the Gender Gap in Science Project

8.1 ISC plans

Lucilla Spini, the International Science Council representative, congratulated warmly the Gender Gap in Science project for its dynamism and results. She insisted on the many "Gender GapS" we have identified in our work e.g., gaps related to publications, salary, continuity in studies, and between disciplines [23].

She presented the international landscape of GEEW (Gender Equality and Empowerment of Women) activities. She concluded with the ISC Action Plan [9], containing a *Project for development* (*Project 4.1 Gender Equality in Science: from awareness to transformation*) directly in line with the Gender Gap in Science project.[2]

Then Marie-Françoise Roy presented the views of the coordination group of the project about the future of the project.

8.2 The situation

The project has been very successful.

First, this has been the first multi-disciplinary project on this topic among professional unions, a very ambitious and challenging collaboration, that has however benefited significantly from sharing information and from the experience in different disciplinary fields.

Second, all the tasks have reached their objectives. Our preliminary report (156 pages long) was distributed for the first time at the final meeting of the project, at ICTP, for discussion. Moreover, we are also planning a short document in several languages to summarize our main findings and recommendations.

Two important tools related to Task 2 and 3 of the project have also been developed:

---

[2]The ISC Action Plan is available online aswell, `https://council.science/actionplan/`.

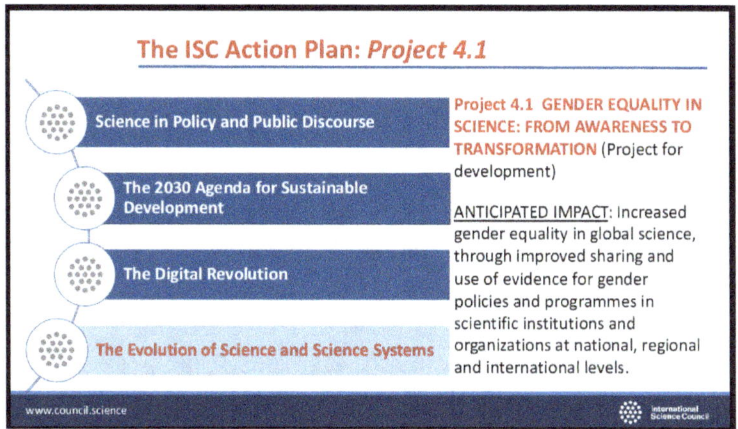

Figure 15: The ISC action plan: *Project 4.1* (slide taken from Lucillia Spini's presentation).

1. The Publication Pattern Task built and maintains an open platform that allows ad hoc analyses of bibliographic data with relation to gender. The resulting webpage can be accessed via its public URL. The site provides structured access to publication data from STEM disciplines in relation to the gender of the publishing authors. The visualizations address several crucial aspects for understanding the impact of publication patterns on the gender gap: research activity over time; share in particular journals; distribution across sub-fields; distribution across sub-fields.[3]

2. A Database of Good Practices, available on IMU Committee for Women in Mathematics (CWM) website, which will be welcoming online submissions of new initiatives.[4]

With respect to the Global Survey of Scientists, the situation is more complex. We have collected a valuable quantity of data but have not been able yet to analyze them fully given

---

[3]Publication pattern study result website,
   http://gender-publication-gap.f4.htw-berlin.de/.
[4]Database of Good Practices website,
   https://www.mathunion.org/cwm/gender-gap-in-science-database.

the project time limits. We have discussed internally how unions and organizations inside or outside the project could access the data and led specific analysis with the data we have collected. The issue is data privacy: individuals who answered the survey must not be identified. The solution initially proposed was to have a committee that would evaluate the proposals and, if approved, hand out the data under certain technical conditions and specific agreements. However those technical requirements are in almost no case guaranteed. Recent technologies ("data suppression technique") make it possible to protect the privacy of data while giving access to researchers, so that we wish to implement them in the future.

8.3 The future

All union and organization representatives in the project want its results and tools to remain available for much longer than the duration of the project. Research questions raised by the project are numerous and dissemination is essential. The partners of the project will be extended to American Institute of Physics and Hochschule für Technik und Wirtschaft Berlin, in order to clarify their role. The partners believe that these results and tools, which are unique if only by the size of the data collected, can open the way for collaboration with the social sciences that are now part of ISC.

It is clear on the other hand that ISC will not be able to extend their funding to our project, which was for three years only.

However, ISC has recently defined its strategic plan and scientific priorities. One of them (4.1) is "Gender-transformative science", in which the following is formulated:

> *"Gender equality in science, is central to the ISC's core values of inclusivity and diversity. It is the focus of work supported directly by the ISC, and an issue of priority concern to most if not all of the Council's members, to its partners and to the broader community of scientists, science policy-makers and funders with whom the Council works. The ISC is uniquely positioned to promote collective gender-transformative actions across the network".* [9]

Moreover, our project is one of the three international initiatives listed as relevant for ISC efforts.

In terms of implementation, "Gender-transformative science" is currently a project for development. ISC plans to co-organize a scoping workshop where our project would be invited to attend and contribute with its main findings.

The Gender Gap in Science project is eager to participate to the scoping workshop planned by ISC.

8.4 How to keep the Gender Gap in Science Project alive?

Our minimal plans for the future are the following:

1. to use current technology ("data suppression technique") in order to provide data access of unions (and individual researchers we would approve) to the Global Survey of Scientists, while protecting the privacy of the respondents to the survey;

2. to organize the long-term availability and maintenance of the tools of the project for Publication Patterns and Data Base of Good Practices.

If we find enough support we would also like

1. to continue research on the open problems identified by the project;

2. to organize dissemination activities through workshops in the developing world;

3. to organize a coordination meeting every year.

The estimated budget is similar to the budget of the project during its three first years. We are contacting private Foundations for financial support. The remaining part of the budget would come from the partner unions and organization through their participation to the coordination meeting.

9 Links

1. To the meeting website and its programme for slide presentations and reports on activities: `http://indico.ictp.it/event/8731/`.

2. to the Youtube channel with the videos of some of the talks: `https://youtube.com/playlist?list=PLLq_gUfXAnknyOAVwNct-WcUtQ_VIk4oZ`.

References

[1] Silvana Badaloni. *Gender In/Equality in Science in Italy*. Presentation slides: `http : / / indico.ictp.it/event/8731/session/11/contribution/17/material/2/`. Nov. 6, 2019.

[2] Tonya Blowers. *Measuring The Gender Gap in STEM*. Presentation slides: `http://indico.ictp.it/event/8731/session/10/contribution/13/material/slides/`, video recording: `https://www.youtube.com/watch?v=vvrfAG_d_C0&t=13m30s`. Nov. 6, 2019.

[3] Camelia Boban. *Gender gap in science in Wikipedia*. Presentation slides: `http://indico.ictp.it/event/8731/session/13/contribution/20/material/slides/`. Nov. 6, 2019.

[4] Jean-Pierre Bourguignon. *Some Data on Gender Issues at the European Research Council*. Presentation slides: `http : / / indico . ictp . it / event / 8731 / session / 11 / contribution/17/material/4/`. Nov. 6, 2019.

[5] Anathea Brooks. *Recent Developments at UNESCO on Gender Equality*. Presentation slides: `http : / / indico . ictp . it / event / 8731 / session / 10 / contribution / 13 / material / slides/`, video recording: `https : / / www . youtube . com / watch ? v = G1WOIf8Npd0`. Nov. 6, 2019.

[6] Tracy Kay Camp. *Changing the Face of Computing*. Presentation slides: `http://indico.ictp.it/event/8731/session/10/contribution/15/material/slides/`, video recording: `https://www.youtube.com/watch?v=fK9-rQXABhA`. Nov. 6, 2019.

[7] Kathryn B. H. Clancy. *The Gender Gap in US STEM is explained by a Gauntlet Problem, Not a Pipeline Problem*. Presentation slides: `http://indico.ictp.it/event/8731/session/11/contribution/17/material/3/`. Nov. 6, 2019.

[8] Erika Coppola. *Gender Equality activities at ICTP*. Video recording: `https : / / www . youtube.com/watch?v=vvrfAG_d_C0`. Nov. 6, 2019.

[9] International Science Council. *Advancing Science as a Global Public Good. Action Plan 2019–2021*. Paris, France: International Science Council, 2019. URL: `https : / / council . science/wp-content/uploads/2019/12/Advancing-Science-as-a-Global-Public-Good_ISC-Action-Plan-landscape.pdf`.

[10] European Commission, Directorate-General for Research and Innovation. *She Figures 2018*. Luxembourg, LU: Publications Office of the European Union, 2019. ISBN: 978-92-79-86715-6. DOI: 10.2777/936.

[11] Merrilyn Goos. *Report on the Data base of good practices*. Presentation slides http://indico.ictp.it/event/8731/session/6/contribution/2/material/slides/, video recording: https://www.youtube.com/watch?v=RsmjNWw85pg. Nov. 5, 2019.

[12] Rachel Ivie and Susan White. *Report on the Global Survey of Scientists*. Presentation slides: http://indico.ictp.it/event/8731/session/2/contribution/0/material/slides/, video recording: https://www.youtube.com/watch?v=1ESeorFd-X4. Nov. 4, 2019.

[13] Catherine Jami. *Some aspects of research on the gender gap in science by social scientists*. Presentation slides: http://indico.ictp.it/event/8731/session/15/contribution/27/material/slides/, video recording: https://www.youtube.com/watch?v=3jcru76Ihog. Nov. 8, 2019.

[14] Guadalupe Lozano. *Present and future: How individuals, policies, institutions, and culture shape the evolving gender gap in science*. Video recording: https://www.youtube.com/watch?v=-pclU7m0Vow. Nov. 8, 2019.

[15] Theodore Melfi (director); Theodore Melfi and Allison Schroeder (writers). *Hidden Figures*. Los Angeles, CA, USA: 20th Century Fox, Dec. 2016.

[16] Helena Mihaljević. *Report on the Joint data-backed study on publication patterns*. Presentation slides: http://indico.ictp.it/event/8731/session/2/contribution/1/material/slides/. Nov. 4, 2019.

[17] Shobhana Narasimhan. *"No longer alone!": Career Development Workshops for Women in Physics*. Presentation slides: http://indico.ictp.it/event/8731/session/10/contribution/33/material/slides/, video recording: https://www.youtube.com/watch?v=SJ8mEfbeE2o. Nov. 6, 2019.

[18] National Academies of Sciences, Engineering, and Medicine. *Sexual Harassment of Women: Climate, Culture, and Consequences in Academic Sciences, Engineering, and Medicine*. Washington, DC, USA: The National Academies Press, 2018. DOI: 10.17226/24994. URL: https://www.nap.edu/catalog/24994/.

Report of the final conference

[19] Marie Françoise Ouedraogo. *What did we learn from the project about the gender gap in science in developed/less developed countries?* Presentation slides: http://indico.ictp.it/event/8731/session/6/contribution/4/material/slides/, video recording: https://www.youtube.com/watch?v=f__aT-GTZG4. Nov. 5, 2019.

[20] Silvina Ponce-Dawson. *What did we learn from the project about the gender gap in science in Asia, Africa, Latin America?* Presentation slides: http://indico.ictp.it/event/8731/session/6/contribution/3/material/slides/, video recording: https://www.youtube.com/watch?v=RPKmIzsJZOI. Nov. 5, 2019.

[21] Petra Rudolf. *Molecular Motors and Switches at Surfaces.* Video recording: https://www.youtube.com/watch?v=A_JYOMq3I_o. Nov. 4, 2019.

[22] Lucía Santamaría. *What did we learn from the project about the gender gap for the various disciplines?* Presentation slides: http://indico.ictp.it/event/8731/session/6/contribution/5/material/slides/, video recording: https://www.youtube.com/watch?v=Q5nhD5F7xsM. Nov. 5, 2019.

[23] Lucilla Spini. *What now? Recommendations of the project.* Presentation slides: http://indico.ictp.it/event/8731/session/17/contribution/32/material/1/, video recording: https://www.youtube.com/watch?v=4d8Hb99hy0Q. Nov. 8, 2019.

[24] Jody Tims. *Gender Gap in Science in North America: A Computer Science Perspective.* Presentation slides: http://indico.ictp.it/event/8731/session/11/contribution/17/material/0/. Nov. 6, 2019.

List of Figures

List of figures

List of Tables